T0330767

The Economics of Feudalism

First published in 1971, *The Economics of Feudalism* is an attempt to use the mathematical theory of economic analysis to analyse a historical society. It also elaborates economic theory to include demographic and political conditions. A specific analysis is made of empire and feudal economies and there are some speculations about their inter-relationships. The foundation and asymptotic properties of the feudal economy are subjected to rough empirical tests from Europe, A.D. 1000-1500. The author has four main theses. With a static agricultural sector and capital accumulation in the towns, urban population falls. Also, the feudal method of organization is a relatively efficient instrument of exploitation for the political dominant class of landlords. Consequently, the terms of trade turn against the towns and in favour of the countryside. Further, where urban wages fall more rapidly than rural wages until they are equal, the feudal system is no longer essential to landowners. This book will be of interest to students of history, economics and agriculture.

The Economics of Feudalism

Trout Rader

Routledge
Taylor & Francis Group

First published in 1971
By Gordon and Breach

This edition first published in 2022 by Routledge
4 Park Square, Milton Park, Abingdon, Oxon, OX14 4RN
and by Routledge
605 Third Avenue, New York, NY 10017

Routledge is an imprint of the Taylor & Francis Group, an informa business

© 1971 Gordon and Breach, Science Publishers, Inc.

Publisher's Note
The publisher has gone to great lengths to ensure the quality of this reprint but points out that some imperfections in the original copies may be apparent.

Disclaimer
The publisher has made every effort to trace copyright holders and welcomes correspondence from those they have been unable to contact.

A Library of Congress record exists under ISBN: 0677032803

ISBN: 978-1-032-44209-9 (hbk)
ISBN: 978-1-003-37103-8 (ebk)
ISBN: 978-1-032-44211-2 (pbk)

Book DOI 10.4324/9781003371038

To Deana, Katherine, and Wendela

THE ECONOMICS OF FEUDALISM

TROUT RADER

Department of Economics
Washington University

GORDON AND BREACH   SCIENCE PUBLISHERS

New York   *London*   *Paris*

MONOGRAPHS AND TEXTS IN THE BEHAVIORAL SCIENCES

This series consists of monographs, textbooks and collections of papers each designed to contribute to interdisciplinary behavioral science. The monographs will report the results of research efforts; the textbooks will summarize the findings of some meaningful area of study in the behavioral sciences; and the collections of papers will bring together previously unpublished papers, or papers that have been published previously, but which need to be brought together in a single volume.

BERNHARDT LIEBERMAN

PREFACE

This book is the completion of work begun in 1965. The motive was to answer John Bowman who questioned the relevance of mathematical theory to the feudal economy. A formal model of the feudal economy was derived from impressions gained in my graduate years at Yale. After the model's implications were set forth, additional empirical research was made. By insight or by luck, the model fitted well to the data available.

The model is one of general market equilibrium. Ideally, a theory based upon coalition structure would be best. However, the present state of game theory is such as to present a bewildering variety of possible solutions without much information about any one. The mechanistic market system of economics is more explored and better understood.

The first chapter is relatively technical and can be omitted in first reading except for sections 1, 3, and 11. In Chapter 1, sections 3–6, 8–10 relate to chapter 2, and sections 3-7, 11, to chapter 3.

I am indebted to correspondence with John Bowman (chapters 2, 3–4), Robert Fogel (chapters 3 and 4), Josiah Russell (chapters 3–5), David Felix (chapters 2–4), Werner Hochwald (chapters 2–4), Leonid Hurwicz (chapters 1 and 3), Ronald Zupko (chapter 3), Joseph Spengler (chapter 2), John Sawyer (chapter 2), and Gordon Tulloch (chapter 2).

I am indebted to my wife for typing, criticism, and encouragement, and to Mrs. Sharon Farley for typing.

TROUT RADER

St. Louis, Missouri

CONTENTS

CHAPTER 1

TOWARD A SOCIO-ECONOMIC THEORY

1 A PREVIEW OF THE METHOD

The main focus of this book is upon the feudal economy, its nature, the causes of its creation, and the reason for its decline. The information available, while less then extensive, will be seen to yield some probable inferences —but only when inserted into formal models of economic, social, and political processes.

A secondary aim of the book is to show how social, economic, and political forces interact. For this purpose, one must have some understanding of production from factors such as labor, natural resources, and capital, and also of the wants and relative values of the people who make up the society. There follows a structure for thought in which certain "parameters" of technology and taste are specified in historical records or inferred indirectly from historical events. There are two possible ways to do this. One is the Econometric method whereby one specifies a theory with variables to "explain" all recorded events and sufficiently simple to be fitted to empirical data so as to determine all parameters. For a period such as Feudalism where the actual quantitative information is sparcely and irregularly distributed over the period, this would appear an almost impossible task. Instead, one can construct a reasonable but quite general picture of the world and then impose certain empirical constraints on the general system. This is the approach of the economic theorist or more precisely of the mathematical economist. "Explanation" is interpreted as the deductive system associated with inductive constraints upon a more or less *a priori* theoretical framework.

2 SOCIO-ECONOMIC SYSTEMS

A *socio-economic system* will be viewed as a dynamical system which assigns to each family or consumer unit various quantities of economic goods, factors of production, and family size depending upon last periods quantities.

1

Symbolically, for every vector x of goods, factors and family size, distinguished family by family, there results a vector, $g(x)$. In general it is not required that $g(x)$ be uniquely determined whereupon there will be a range of possible values. In this case, there is a set of vectors, $G(x)$, representing the plausible states of the world resulting from x.

As an example, under *pure competition*, there is a price system presented to the consumers by which they are required to choose only those economic goods whose summed value does not exceed their income from productive activities plus the value of their initial wealth. The price system covers both goods for current use and for future use. The families project their family size and their activities, in order to obtain the highest possible benefit for the current generation subject to the budget constraint. There results current consumptions and activities (as well as prospective future ones). The next generation finds itself with the last periods resources and family size as modified by the preceding generation. Provided the tastes of the second generation are identical to those of the first, the second will always choose just like the first given the same situation. However, the situation is not generally preserved over time. Families become richer or poorer, larger or smaller, and the photograph of the economy proceeds according to the law $G^n(x)$ which equals the set of x^n such that there exists

$$x^i, i = 0, 1, \ldots, n,$$

x^i is in $G(x^{i-1})$ for all $i > 0$ and $x^0 = x$. Since G is independent of time, it is said that the socio-economic system is *invariant over time*.

At the abstract level, the most interesting properties of G are limiting ones as time tends to infinity. It is said that x^i *tends* to x if the difference between x and x^i in each component tends to zero. x^i *tends frequently* to x if there is a subsequence x^{ij} tending to x. For example, $\frac{1}{2}, \frac{1}{4}, \ldots$ tends to zero whereas $1, \frac{1}{2}, 1, \frac{1}{4}, 1, \frac{1}{8}, \ldots$ frequently tends to zero. x is *quasi-recurrent* if there is *some* time path from x, x^i in $G(x^{i-1})$, $x^0 = x, i = 1, 2, \ldots$, such that x^i tends frequently to x. A more stringent case is recurrence: x is *recurrent* if for *every* time path from x, x^i in $G(x^{i-1})$, $x^0 = x, i = 1, 2, \ldots$, x^i tends frequently to x. x is *cyclic* of order n if for *every* time path from x, $x^n = x$ for all x^n in $G^n(x)$. If x is cyclic, then also x is recurrent. For example, there is a theory of civilization which says that every social order contains the seeds of its own downfall. Contiguous areas take its place as centers of prosperity and "westward the cause of empire takes its way." Since the populated world is a cylinder, prosperity eventually returns to any former location with the establishment of a new social system and a consequent decay. Strictly interpreted, the theory says that the socio-economic system is cyclic, at least in some of its components. Less strictly interpreted, the socio-economic system is recurrent.

In contrast the system may tend to several states of affairs which are cyclic or recurrent instead of being recurrent itself. In effect, one judges the properties of limiting states by their paths in a post-time which should be similar to the paths in the latter days of the system. A particular case is that where the x^t tends to a y such that y is in $G(y)$ (i.e. y is quasi *cyclic* of order one). In this case, y is a *quasi-stationary state*. If $y = G(y)$, y is a *stationary* state.

One theory says that civilization evolves to a final and perfect state: "Westward the course of empire takes its way; / a fifth shall close the drama with the day; / time's noblest offspring is the last." Along similar lines, Malthus predicted that population explosion would engulf the world in starvation driving consumption to the subsistence level where population was stationary. An ultimately more pleasant prospect was prophesized by Marx. He predicted that at least the working class would be driven to subsistence due to the invention of labor saving devices and the desire of the capitalist class to have cheap labor. In the view of Marx, the decline of the working class would trigger a revolution of the proletariat and move the system into its final and blissful stationary state.

Some mathematical properties will be needed to insure that x^t frequently tends to a recurrent state. Eventually, there will appear conditions under which it tends to a stationary state. Of paramount importance are various continuity properties of G. It is said that G is a *correspondence* whenever $G(x)$ has multiple elements (Otherwise, if $G(x)$ has always one element, G is a *function*). G is *upper semi-continuous* if "$x^n \to x$, y^n in $G(x)^n$, $y^n \to y$" imply y is in $G(x)$. In words, limits of paths starting from x^n are paths starting from limit x^n. Said differently, the graph of G is closed. This is illustrated schematically in Figure 1. Note that G in Figure 1 is a function between x and $\bar{x}$ but not after $\bar{x}$ or before x. In general, G in figure 1 is a correspondence and its graph as presented contains all its limiting points, whereupon its graph is a closed set.

G is *lower semi-continuous* if "y in $G(x)$, x^n tends to x" imply that there are y^n in $G(x^n)$ such that y^n tends to y. In words, for any given path and for every sequence of starting points tending to that starting point of the path, there are paths whose limit is the given path. This is illustrated in Figure 2, where G is lower semi-continuous but not continuous. (In Figure 2, points along the dotted boundary of the graph of $G(x)$ are not in the graph of G). Note that in Figure 1, G is not lower semi-continuous since points tending

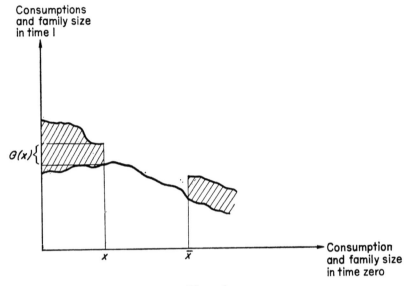

Figure 1

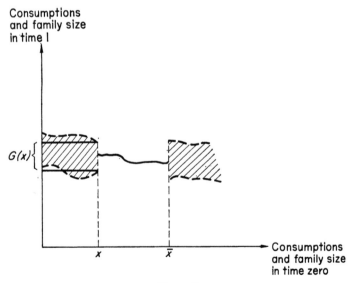

Figure 2

to *x* from the right have no paths to correspond to most of the paths from *x*. In Figure 2, $G(x)$ has only one point and is the limit of paths from either side of *x*, but there are limiting paths from nearby initial points without corresponding paths from *x*. A path $(x^i, i = 1, 2, ...)$ is *bounded* if there is some number such that no component of x^i exceeds it in absolute value that number. A path is *frequently bounded* if there are i_j tending to infinity and a number such that no components of x^{i_j} exceed in absolute value that number. If there is a limiting resource, such as land, then wealth, economic goods and family sizes are bounded (even though the bounds may be very remote from everyday experience).

1 THEOREM

If G is upper semi-continuous and paths from x are bounded, there is at least one path which tends frequently to a quasi recurrent point. If G is lower semi-continuous and all paths from x are frequently bounded, then there is a path from x tending frequently to a recurrent point.

(One can imagine stronger theorems, giving recurrent or cyclic points, but at this level of generality, such results are not to be had). For application to a socio-economic system, one must verify the continuity properties. The proof requires some rather deep mathematical results.

Proof 1 *G upper semi-continuous* A set, *A*, is *quasi-invariant*, if for every *x* in *A* there exists a path, x^i, $i = 1, 2, ..., x^1$ in $G(x^{i-1})$ and x^i in *A*.

It is easy to show that the intersection of quasi invariant sets is quasi-invariant. Also, the closure of quasi-invariant set is quasi-invariant.* Let x^i be in $G^i(x(n))$ and in *A*, $x(n) \to x$. The proof is by induction. For $j < i$, we can take a convergent subsequence, $x^i(n_k)$ tending to x^i (a convergent subsequence exists because for all *x*, $G^i(x)$ is in a bounded set). Therefore, upper semi-continuity applies: x^i is in $G(x^{i-1})$ and hence is in $G^i(x^0) = G^i(x)$. Since each $x^i(n_k)$ is in *A*, x^i is in the closure of *A*, $1 = 0, 1, ...,$

We can apply the Brouwer reduction theorem to the bounded set in which the path from *x* must remain. Inside any closed quasi invariant set there is a closed quasi-invariant set which contains no proper closed quasi-invariant set. Such a set is called *minimal*. Evidently, for any *x*, a path x^i, $i = 1, 2, ..., x^i$ in $G(x^{i-1})$ is quasi invariant as is its closure. Therefore, any such path contains a minimal closed quasi invariant set. Such a set

---

* The closure of a set is the set itself and all points which are limits of sequences of points from the set.

contains paths from any point in it, and must be the closure of any path in it. Hence, any point in it must be quasi recurrent for if not, for large n, x^i is not near x^0, $i > n$ and the closure of x^n, does not contain x^0, whereupon it is a closed quasi invariant proper subset.

2 *G lower semi-continuous* A set A, is *invariant* if for every x in A, $G(x)$ is contained in A. It is easy to show that the intersection of invariant sets is invariant. Also the closure of invariant sets is invariant. To see this, let $x(n)$ be in A, $x(n)$ tending to x. Then if y is in $G(x)$, there are $y(n)$ in $G(x(n))$, $y(n)$ tending to y (lower semi-continuity). Since $y(n)$ is in A, y is in the closure of A.

There is an appropriate modification of the Brouwer reduction theorem for the case where every path is frequently bounded. The set of points in $G^i(x)$ from some $i \geq 0$ is called an *orbit* from x. An orbit is invariant as is its closure. Also, any sub orbit closure contains points within the bound. The set of all such points is closed and the Brouwer reduction theorem applies. There is an orbit closure not properly contained in any other having points within the bound. Clearly, there can be no smaller closed invariant subset. Since each invariant set contains all orbits starting from x, there is a path tending frequently to x. Each orbit closure contains a minimal orbit closure which contains a quasi-recurrent point.

q.e.d.

For more details on continuity of correspondences, the reader is referred to Berge, *Topological Spaces and Multi-Valued Functions*.

3 THE HIERARCHY OF ETHICS

Socio-economic systems are judged by the efficiency with which they obtain desired goals. At the very least, they are measured by the goals to which they profess to adhere. An output is *producer efficient* if there is no other feasible output giving at least as much of all commodities and more of one. A distribution of output among consumers is *trade efficient* if given the output, there is no way of redistributing it so as to make one consumer better off without hurting others. An output and its distribution are *consumer efficient* if there is no other output with a distribution which makes one consumer better off without hurting any others. More generally, one output and/or distribution is (producer, trade, consumer) superior to another if it offers more (of, to) one without giving less (of, to) another.

An output and a distribution are *equitable* if two families with the same wealth, abilities, and tastes are treated equally well. An output and a distribution are *consumer conservative* if no consumer or group of consumers is made worse off than they would be on the basis of their own wealth and abilities.

Consumer efficiency implies trade efficiency, if no commodities are undesirable to hold or if they can be utilized as intermediate products to obtain desirable commodities. Consumer conservative implies consumer efficiency since the set of all consumers is one particular group. Where there are two or more identical copies of each type of family, consumer conservation implies equity.

A trade-production which is producer inefficient would invite social action to produce more to meet social goals. A distribution which was trade inefficient would invite new trading arrangements to obtain an efficient distribution. If production and trade are efficient, it does not necessarily follow that there is consumer efficiency. The output must not only be distributed efficiently but it must have the right mix of commodities. Hence, consumer inefficiency may not be correctable by the going social order. In such a case, peaceful revolution (or evolution) of social institutions would see imminent, more or less supported by a consences of opinion. If a production and distribution is not consumer conservative, and if this state of affairs persists, it would seem that the injured parties would be the source of constant unrest, even if they had not the means for successful revolution.

4 PRODUCER EFFICIENCY

It is assumed that there are n industries producing n goods from m factors. The goods and factors are distinguished as to location, e.g. soap in Bruges, carriage transport from London to Bristol, etc. For concreteness, let factors quantities be denoted $y(t)$ in time t, $y(t)$ a vector with m components, and let (net) outputs be denoted $x(t)$, a vector with n components. In any given time period factors are fixed in quantity. Over time, they are accumulated and/or deteriorate at rates which cannot be controlled except through production from other factors. Some of the coordinates of $x(t)$ refer to increments in factors. Other commodities may also accumulate and deteriorate. Their stocks can be denoted $z(t)$, a vector with $m - n$ components. Hence, both factors and non-factors are both referred to as commodity stocks of which there are n, $(y(t), z(t))$. There is the law: $(y(t + 1), z(t + 1))$

$= (y(t), z(t)) + x(t)$. One path of commodity stocks would be producer superior to another if in any time period it gave at least as much of all commodity stocks as the other and for some period, and for some commodity stock, it gave more. Formally, $\hat{c} = (\hat{y}(t), \hat{z}(t), t = 0, 1, ...)$ is producer superior to $c = (y(t), z(t)\, t = 0, 1, ...)$, if $\hat{c} \geq c$ but $\hat{c} \neq c$. It would follow that whenever the two started from the same initial quantities of commodity stocks, there would be a first time period such that one was superior, i.e. a first time for which

$$(\hat{y}(t), \hat{z}(t)) \geq (y(x), z(x)),$$

but

$$(\hat{y}(t), \hat{z}(t)) \neq (y(t), z(t)).$$

In the preceding time period, both had the same factors (and other commodity stocks) and since only production can overcome the natural forces of deterioration, the one must have produced more. The other utilizes its inputs inefficiently at that time. Formally,

$$(\hat{y}(t), \hat{z}(t)) = (y(t-1), z(t-1)) + \hat{x}(t-1)$$

$$\geq (y(t), z(t)) = (y(t-1), z(t-1)) + x(t-1),$$

and therefore,

$$(\hat{y}(t), \hat{z}(t) - (y(t), z(t))$$

$$= \hat{x}(t) - x(t) \geq 0.$$

2   REMARK

Producer efficiency over time results if and only if there is producer efficiency in each time period separately. All results following will refer only to the given time period although they are related to the case of factors variable over time. The time notation is dropped and there appear only the variables, factor inputs, y and net outputs, x.

Production is *inter-industry* if there are the following conditions:

1) Commodities are produced in industries by production functions $f^i(y^i)$, where y^i is the vector of the quantities of factors used in the ith industry and $f^i(y^i)$ is the amount of the ith good produced, net in the industry but gross in the economy. It is required that f^i be continuous, i.e. small decreases in inputs lead to small decreases in outputs. (It is possible that in producing the ith good, certain other goods are produced in negative quan-

tities indicating their use as raw materials or intermediate products. If more than two goods are produced in positive quantities, they are joint outputs).

2) For the community, the *net output*, x, is obtained by summing industry outputs, x^i, which are vectors including the negative quantities representing the use of intermediate products. In equations,

$$x = \Sigma x^i$$

and

$$x_i^i = f^i(y^i).$$

If the intermediate products are not subtracted from the total, the summation over industries gives *gross output*. It will be required that no increase in all net outputs can be attained simultaneously with decreasing outputs in some industry. Therefore, one cannot increase the quantity of j produced in industry i and also reduce the raw materials requirements or the output of joint products. Therefore, $|x_j^i|$ is a non-decreasing function of $x_{i\cdot}^i$.

3) Hereafter, the word factor of production is applied only to producer goods, namely those which can be utilized to produce some good in some industry. It is assumed that small increases in factors lead to small increases in output.

Summarizing,

$$x_i^i = f^i(y^i), \tag{1}$$

$$x^i = x^i(x_i^i), \tag{2}$$

$$x = \Sigma x^i, \tag{3}$$

$$y = \Sigma y^i. \tag{4}$$

An example of (2) is the Leontief system where,

$$x^i = B^i x_i^i,$$

B^i a vector of n constants.

Productions is *quasi-concave* provided the production functions are quasi-concave:

$$f^i(ty^i + (1 - t)\, \bar{y}^i) \geqq \min\left(f(y^i), f(\bar{y}^i)\right)$$

whenever $0 \leqq t \leqq 1$. In Figure 3, there are iso-output curves for various amounts of capital and labor. Along such a curve, there are labor, capital quantities given the same gross output. The meaning of quasi-concavity is that the iso-product curves (or hyper surfaces) are convex to the origin. In effect, as the quantity of j increases, the slope of the iso-product curve equals the marginal rate of substitution of i for j, when defined, is not increasing in absolute value (not decreasing in actual value). This does not exclude increasing, constant, or decreasing returns to scale since the returns to scale are determined by the distance between the isoproduct curves (hyper surfaces).

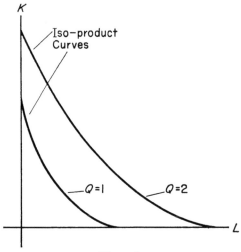

Figure 3

Factors are productive in an industry whenever their increase increases output in that industry. Production is *factor-connected* if for any industries i and k, there are industries q_m, $m = 1, ..., p$, and factors $j(q_m)$ such that

$$q_1 = i,$$

$$q_p = k,$$

and $j(q_m), j(q_{m=1})$ are utilized in positive quantities and are productive in the q_mth industry. For example, every industry produces a positive (gross) output.

To see the meaning of factor connected, consider the case where production is not factor connected. If by changing the order of industries or factors, we have a matrix

$$(y_j^i) = \begin{pmatrix} A & 0 \\ 0 & B \end{pmatrix},$$

then production is not factor connected. Industries can be divided into two groups who use no factors in common. For example, there might be two industries, steel and coal, the one using only capital and the other only labor. Suppose there is idle capacity in steel because of an insufficient supply of coal, which goes into steel as an intermediate product. Then output of steel could be increased but only if less coal were available for other uses. A situation with idle steel capacity is efficient because more steel requires less coal, net. This state of affairs would make a theory of efficiency quite cumbersome.

3 THEOREM

If production is inter-industry, factor-connected, and quasi-concave, then a net output is producer efficient if and only if there is a strictly positive wage system, w, such that each industry i maximizes its gross output subject to wy^i constant.

The implications of theorem 3 for planned or slave economics might be mentioned, since Soviet type economies often assign factors to industries instead of allowing them to circulate freely according to market laws. To allow industries to trade factors among themselves could assure efficiency without going the whole way to allowing factors to choose the industry in which they are employed. Also, for planned economics, it would be useful to know that whatever the initial factor holdings, there is an equilibrium system of factor wages. This follows from the Arrow-Debreu existence theorem, provided the production functions are continuous.* Existence is not proved here and hence it is not listed as a theorem, although it can be deduced from theorem 13 below.

4 LEMMA

If production is inter-industry and factor-connected, then in each industry production is maximized with respect to a strictly positive wage system and a budget constraint on factors if and only if all factors are employed and factor costs are minimized with respect to a strictly positive wage system and a constant output constraint.

Proof If greater output were possible with the same cost, a reduction in factors could take place for the industry and reduce costs without reducing output below its original level. Said differently, production is maximized subject to a factor cost constraint whenever costs are minimized and all factors are fully employed.

---

* Arrow and Debreu, "Existence of Equilibrium for a Competitive Economy," *Econometrica*, 22 (1954), 265–29.

On the other hand, factors are fully employed whenever firms trade factors among themselves and maximize output since unemployed factors would be offered for sale. Also, were it possible to produce at lesser cost the same output, the difference could be used to obtain appropriate factors and increase output. Hence, maximizing production implies minimizing costs.

q.e.d.

5 THEOREM

If production is inter-industry, factor-connected, and quasi-concave, a net output is producer efficient if and only if there is full employment of factors and the gross outputs minimize costs of each industry subject to a fixed output constraint with respect to a strictly positive wage system.

Theorem 5 applies to private enterprise economics where there are monopolies. So long as the monopolies take factor wages as given, there is no producer inefficiency (although there may be consumer inefficiency). Contrariwise, Collective bargaining or guild restrictions with differential wages for the same factor lead to producer inefficiency.

In view of lemma 4, theorems 3 and 5 are logically equivalent. The proof of theorem 5 is standard procedure in classical welfare economics.

Proof Sufficiency:

If a net output, $\bar{x}$, exceeds x in one or more goods and is not less than x for any good, then also the intermediate products used and the gross output is larger for $\bar{x}$ than for x. Hence, each industry is producing at a higher level. Since $wy^i \neq 0$ for industry i having a greater output in $\bar{x}$ than in x, $wy^i > wy^i$. (If not, cut down on factor inputs without reducing output to a level below that in x, which gives a lower cost of production than wy). In the same way, for all other industries, $w\bar{y}^j \geq wy^j$. By summation, $w\bar{y} > wy$, whereupon $\bar{y} \leq y$ is impossible. Only by having greater imputs can one attain greater net output.

Necessity:

For good i, the set of factors producing more of i than the output in the efficient x is denoted F_i. Clearly, F_i is a convex set as is ΣF_i. Also, ΣF_i cannot contain $y = \Sigma y^i$ since that would mean that one could use y to obtain more of all goods gross. By an appropriate transferral of factors to other industries, one can provide for both an increase in the net output of goods and the added raw material requirements (factor connectivity). Therefore, one would have a larger net output.

We can apply Minkowski's theorem: there is a vector w such that $w\Sigma F_i \geqq wy$. Since y^i is in the boundary of F_i, $wF_i + \sum\limits_{i \neq j} wy^j \geqq wy^j$ for all j.

Since small increases in a productive factor increase output, any input with the same output is in the boundary of F_j, so that again it is no cheaper than y.

Because increases in factors increase production in some industry, w is non-negative. It can easily be shown that a zero wage for one factor can lead to a lower cost of the same output. Simply substitute the factor with zero wage for one with positive wages. By factor connectivity, there will be some industry in which this is possible.

q.e.d.

For quasi-concave production, marginal rates of substitution are defined almost everywhere in the factor space.

6 Theorem

If production is inter-industry, factor connected, and quasi-concave and with marginal rates of substitution defined with respect to all factors used, then a net output with strictly positive gross outputs is producer efficient if and only if

1) *all factors are employed*
2) *all marginal rates of substitution of factors used are equal between industries, and*
3) *all marginal rates of substitution of used factors to unused factors are at least that in industries where both factors are used.*

Evidently, differential wages in some but not all factors leads to inefficiency.

Proof The necessity is immediate from theorem 5 and the observation that cost minimization with respect to w leads to equality of the marginal rates of substitution of j for k is equal to w_j/w_k whenever both factors are used. Otherwise, if j is not used, the marginal rate of substitution must not exceed w_j/w_k.

Sufficiency follows from the fact that a wage vector can be formed from the equality of marginal rates of substitution, by letting $w_i = 1$ and then deducing the other wages as equal to the marginal rate of substitution of factors used in conjunction with i, etc. They will be all non-negative and for factors actually used, the wages will be positive. Hence, the wages will define a hyperplane equal to the set of $\bar{y}^i$ for which $y^i w = yw$ which is tangent to F_i at x^i. Since F_i is convex, the hyperplane must bound F_i, and the industry minimizes costs with respect to w.

q.e.d.

5 DISTRIBUTION AND TRADE

On the consumer side, families are assumed to rank vectors of present and future commodities. If among two such vectors, x and y, y is preferred to x by family i, then xP_iy. If y and x are indifferent, then xI_iy, and if xI_iy or xP_iy, then xR_iy (x is not inferior to y).

Such a ranking is illustrated in Figure 4, where the curves represent points of indifference, denoted $I_i(x)$. The set of superior alternatives is denoted

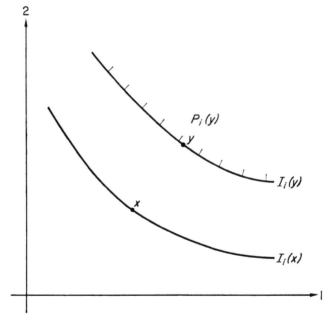

Figure 4

$P_i(y)$. When defined, the slope of the indifference curve is the marginal rate of substitution, exactly as in the production from factors.

Under certain circumstances, there is a utility function, u^i such that $u^i(x)$

$\geq u^i(y)$ if and only if xR_iy.* In particular, if $I_i(x)$ is a closed set which bounds $P_i(x)$, there is a continuous (gross) utility function, u_i. Evidently, u_i is quasi-concave if and only if $P_i(x)$ are convex sets. If u_i is non-decreasing in each commodity, we have an analogy with production. Preferences are *consumer connected* if for every pair of consumers, k and 1, there are consumers q_m, $m = 1, ..., p$, $q_1 = k$, $q_p = l$ and consumers q, n, q_{m+1} hold commodities useful to each other.

7 Theorem

If

a) *output is allocated to families*
b) *every commodity is useful to some family and no commodity is of negative value*
c) *among those consumer for which $u(x^i) > u^i(0)$, preferences are consumer connected.*
d) *u_i is continuous, and quasi-concave*
e) *if $u^i(x^i) = u^i(0)$ and i has increasing utility in good, k, then there is some consumer j with $u^i(x^i) > u^i(0)$ who also desires k.*

Then there is trade efficiency if and only if any of the three following equivalent conditions hold:

1) *Consumers maximize utility subject to a constant expenditure constraint with respect to strictly positive price system,*
2) *Consumers minimize costs of the budget subject to a constant utility constraint—with respect to a strictly positive price systems, or*
3) *for goods consumed, the marginal rates of substitution are equal and otherwise, the marginal rates of substitution for i of an unused commodity relative to a used one is less than that for j consuming both.*

The proof is by analogy with theorems 3, 5, and 6. Actually, the state of affairs is a little simpler in that there are no intermediate products. Indeed, one can do considerably better than theorem 7, allowing for waste products

---

* Rader, "Existence of a Utility Function to Represent Preferences," *Review of Economic Studies*, 30, (1963), 299–232, and Debreu, "Continuity Properties of Paretion Utility," *International Economic Review*, 5, (1964), 235–93.

with negative prices.* However, this would be far afield and theorem 11
appears to be adquate for present purposes.

Condition 1) gives that there is trade efficiency if and only if there is a
competitive equilibrium trade. As before, the existence of competitive
equilibrium is assured under the given continuity and quasi-concavity
conditions.† Hypothesis 3) can be shown to give that there is trade efficiency
if and only if each consumer attains any mutually advantageous trade with
any other.‡

Consumers with $u^i(x^i) = 0$ would include those who were slaves. § For
them, integration into the competitive economy might be impossible. An
example due to Arrow is as follows. Suppose there is a farmer who grows
wheat and suppose wild onions grow on the unused portions of his land. A
second consumer who is a pauper lives off the meager supply of onions
which the farmer gives him free, since given that he has an adequate supply
of wheat, the farmer has no use for wild onions. There is no way to put a
price on onions to integrate it with the wheat market. Any positive price of
onions in terms of wheat cannot be paid by the pauper. At a zero price, the
pauper will demand a somewhat larger quantity than the available supply.
This situation can be resolved by assuming that paupers' obtain utility only
from goods which at least some non-pauper enjoys: In effect, paupers must
be slaves.

Proof In view of theorems 3, 5, 6, only the case of slaves need by considered. Since $u^i(x^i) = 0$, $px^i = 0$ by (e) and the fact that prices are positive
for goods desirable among non-paupers. Also, any preferred consumption
involves more of some good desired by non-slaves. Hence, $p\bar{x}^i > px^i$ for
$u^i(\bar{x}^i) > u^i(x^i)$.

q.e.d.

This is the classical invisible hand, effecting the public welfare through
selfish means—as taught by Adam Smith. In the absence of quasi-concavity

---

* See Arrow "An Extension of the Basic Theorems of Classical Welfare Economics,"
  in Neyman, ed. *Proceedings of the Second Berkeley Symposium*, California, 1951,
  507–532, Debreu, "Valuation Equilibrium and Pareto Optimum, "*Proceedings of the
  National Academy of Sciences of the U.S.A.*, 40, (1953), 588–592 and Rader, "Pairwise
  Optimality and Non-competive Behavior," in Quirk and Zarley, eds., *Papers in
  Quantitative Economics*, Vol I, University of Kansas.

† Arrow and Debreu, *op. cit.* and Rader, *op. cit.*

‡ See Rader; *op. cit.*

§ Theodore Bergstrom, "Existence and Optimality of Slave Equilibrium," mimeographed, 1969.

of preferences, there may still be enough consumers with virtually identical preferences so that the above theory works to an approximation. This is an outstanding conjecture in welfare economics.*

6 CONSUMERS EFFICIENCY

We could now move into some asymptotic results about invariant socio-economics. Instead, this is deferred to the later sections and the question of efficiency when both production and distribution are at stake is considered. The nature of the problem can be seen by reference to Figure 5, where there are two goods and one consumer. The output set is the set of

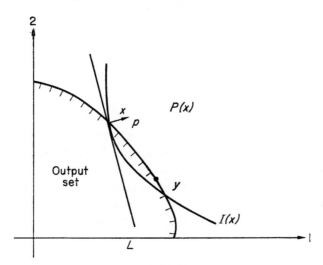

Figure 5

vectors of goods attainable from the given factors of production. The point x is the chosen output and it is producer efficient. Clearly, utility is maximized among z for which $\Sigma p_i z_i = \Sigma p_i x_i$. The equation is the budget constraint where $p = (p_1, p_2)$ is normal to the line L tangent to $I(x)$. Hence, x is trade efficient. (Actually, since there is one consumer, this is trivial to verify). Nevertheless, x is not consumer efficient since y is still better and is within the output set.

---

* See Starr, "Quasi Equilibria in markets with Non-Convex Preferences," *Econometrica*, 37, (1969), 15–24, and Rader, problem E of Chapter 4 of *Theory of General Economic Equilibrium*, forthcoming, Academic Press.

In the case of a convex output set consumer efficiency requires maximization of the value of net output, $\Sigma p_i x_i$, which is called GNP, which is illustrated in Figure 6.

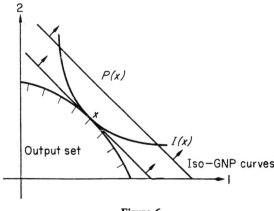

Figure 6

In many cases, under increases returns in several of the industries, the production set is not convex, as illustrated in Figure 7, where industry 2 displays increasing returns. The consumer still chooses according to a budget constraint, but GNP is no longer maximized. Nevertheless, the line L is tangent to the output set. The line L' is also tangent to the output set and has the same relative prices as L. Evidently, $\bar{x}$ is not consumer efficient even

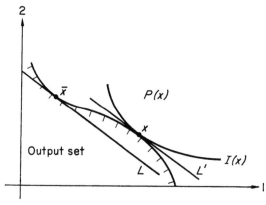

Figure 7

though, as shall be seen, price equals marginal cost. Price equals marginal cost and competitive consumer choice are not sufficient for consumer efficiency. Returning to the case of a convex output set, simply observe that under increasing returns there will be convexity if the loss of scale from the less intense operation of increasing returns industries is more than offset by economies of rearranging the proportions in which resources are used. In contrast if there is but one factor of production, increasing returns is incompatable with the convexity of the output set.

It is easy to see that x is consumer efficient if and only if the output set is disjoint from the set $\Sigma P_i(x^i)$. To establish the rule price equals marginal cost, it is necessary to have uniqueness of the consumer price system at x given budget hyper surfaces bounding each $P_i(x^i)$ at x^i. This follows whenever for every y not in the bounding hyperplane, there is a $t \neq 0$ (possibly negative) such that ty is in $\Sigma P_i(x^i)$. In words, in the direction of production with greater GNP, there is a small change which can be distributed so as to improve the position of all consumers. In this case, it is said that $\Sigma P_i(x^i)$ is *directional dense*.

Production is *continuously differentiable* if all f^i are continuously differentiable.

8 THEOREM

If $\Sigma P_i(x^i)$ is directional dense, if the competitive consumer price system is p, and if production is inter-industry, factor-connected, quasi-concave, and continuously differentiable, then for a consumer efficient production with all products produced, there is a strictly positive wage system, w such that

1) *industries minimize costs subject to the constant output constraint,*
2) $p(dx^j/dx_j^j) (\partial f^j/\partial y_k^j) \leqq w_k$ *with equality whenever y^k is used in positive quantities in industry j and*
3) $p_j = -\sum\limits_{j \neq i} p_j \, dx_i^i/dx_i^i + dwy^j/dq^j$ *(price equals marginal cost).*

Note that (2) and full employment of factors are sufficient for producer efficiency.

Proof Use the wage system of theorem 8 and let

$$p(dx^i/dx_i^i) (\partial f^i/\partial y_k^i) = p\partial x^i/\partial y_k^i = w_k$$

whenever $y_k^i > 0$. It is easy to see that this multiplies w by a positive constant. It is also easy to see that in the limit, small changes in output must have values which tend to non-positive numbers. For industries i and j with continuously differentiable $f^i . f^j$, for $y_k^i > 0$, $y_k^i > 0$, we can either transfer factor k from i to j or from j to i, so that the curve of change in net outputs must be tangent to the separating hyperplane. Hence,

$$p \, \partial x^i/\partial y_k^i - p \, \partial x^j/\partial y_k^j = 0$$

or

$$p \, \partial q^i/\partial y_k^i = w_k$$

For

$$y_k^i \neq 0$$

and

$$y_k^i = 0,$$

$$w_k = p \, \partial x^i/\partial y_k^i \geqq p \, \partial x^j/\partial y_j^j$$

Also,

$$p \, dx^i/dx_i = \Sigma_k p \, \partial x^i/\partial y_k \, dy_k/dq_i = \Sigma_k w_k \, dy_k^i/dq_i$$

gives value added equals marginal cost. Transferring raw materials costs to the other side of the equation, we have the price equals marginal cost rule, (3).

q.e.d.

9   REMARK

In theorem 8,

$$p \, \partial x^i/\partial y_k \leqq aw_k$$

and

$$p_j + \sum_{j \neq i} p_j \, dx_j^j/dx^i = a \, dwy^j/dx_j^j$$

can be substituted in 2) and 3), $a > 0$. Hence, factors of production need not be paid their marginal value products. It is necessary only that industries act as if they were paying the factors their marginal products.

Proof   If

$$p_j + \sum_{j \neq i} p_j f x_j^j/dx_i^i = a \, dwy^j/dx_j^j,$$

we can simply increase wage to aw and apply theorem 8.

q.e.d.

Remark 9 establishes a conjecture of Lerner.* It suggests the possibility of attaining optimality by equalizing the "degree" of monopoly over the economy by assuring everywhere the equality of average value added with marginal factor costs. Simply tax competitive industries and subsidize monopolistic ones. Adjust the rates so that

---

* Lerner, *The Economics of Control*, 1946, Chapter 9.

1) value added bears the same proportion to marginal costs in all industries. The proportion may be any positive number, chosen so that

2) total government revenues equal total government subsidies. If desired, another tax-subsidy scheme on factor incomes can be used to attain the distribution of income under pure competition. Incidentally, there are good welfare reasons for desiring the competitive distribution of benefits, as shall be seen.

One case considered by Marshall is that where an industry has non constant returns to scale but they are external to the firm. The firms can be pure competitors, and price equals industry marginal cost can be attained by an appropriate tax-subsidy scheme. The case of Cobb-Douglas production functions has been treated by Chipman.* In general, let there be n identical firms with marginal factor costs equal to average industry factor costs, AC. Let industry marginal factor costs be MC. Then the firms set average value added $(1 + \text{Subsidy rate}) = AC$ which gives, for average value added $= MC$, gives

$$\frac{AC}{1 + \text{subsidy rate}} = MC, \text{ or}$$

$$\text{subsidy rate} = \frac{AC}{MC} - 1.$$

If output is homogeneous of degree n, $n\,MC = AC$ or subsidy rate $= n - 1$, which is the classical result.

10   COROLLARY

With competitive choice, a larger GNP is necessary but not sufficient for a consumer superior outputs and distributions.

The reasons for insufficiency can be illustrated in Figure 7 above by drawing the indifference curve tangent to $\bar{x}$ instead of x.

In the case of a convex production set, profit maximization and price equals marginal cost and the equality of the marginal rates of substitution are sufficient as well as necessary for consumer efficiency. In the case of concave production functions, this can be read into theorem 7 by assigning production sets to families and considering the utility from trades to be induced from production and then consumption.† It will turn out that the

---

* Lipman, "External Economics of Scale and Competition Equilibrium," *Quarterly T. of Economics*, **84**, (1970), 347–383.

† Rader, "Edgeworth Exchange and General Economic Equilibrium," *Yale Economic Essays*, 1963, 133–180.

induced utility is quasi-concave whenever the original utility is quasi-concave and the production functions are concave. More generally, there is an optimum if and only if the output set is disjoint from $\Sigma P(x^i)$, whereupon there is a separating hyperplane through x with $\Sigma P(x^i)$ to one side and the output set to the other. In case of directional density, the hyperplane is exactly the unique hyperplane bounding $\Sigma P(x^i)$.

11 THEOREM

If $\Sigma P_i(x^i)$ is directional dense, prices p are strictly positive, and the output set is convex, then x is consumer efficiency if and only if Σx^i maximizes GNP with respect to p.

Proof $py > px$ would mean that the output set were not below the hyperplane.

q.e.d.

12 COROLLARY

If $\Sigma P_i(x^i)$ is directional dense, prices p are strictly positive, the output set is convex, and production is factor connected, and continuously differentiable, then x is consumer efficient for the commodities produced in positive quantities if and only if

1) *all factors are employed*
2) *price equals marginal cost*
3) *all marginal rates of substitution of factors used are equal between industries, and*
4) *all marginal rates of substitution of used factors to unused factors are at least that in industries where both factors are used.*

The assumption of directional density is unnecessarily strong, but to weaken it makes a rather long story.* The theorem refers only to the set of commodities in positive production. The problem of new or obsolete products is a more complicated issue.†

Proof Let y^i_j be the inputs of type j in industry i used in producing x and $\bar{y}^i_j$ be the inputs of type j in industry i used to produce $\bar{x}$ for any other $\bar{x}$ in the output set. If the production functions are concave, then price equals marginal cost and cost minimization given output are equivalent to profit maximization. Hence, for z^i the gross outputs of

---

* Rader, *op. cit.*, Chapter 2.

† Chipman, John, "The Nature and Meaning of Equilibrium in Economic Theory," in *Functionalism in the Social Sciences*, American Academy of Political and Social Science, Philadelphia, 1965, 35–64.

industry i (in producing x),

$$pz^i - wy^i \geq p\bar{z}^i - w\bar{y}^i$$

where $\bar{z}^i$ is produced from $\bar{y}^i$ (in producing $\bar{x}$). Hence,

$$\Sigma pz^i - \Sigma wy^i = p\Sigma z^i - wy \geq p\Sigma\bar{z}^i - wy = \Sigma p\bar{z}^i - \Sigma w\bar{y}^i$$

or subtracting wy from both sides

$$px = p\Sigma z^i \geq p\Sigma\bar{z}^i = p\bar{x}$$

and x maximizes GNP. Apply theorem 11.

q.e.d.

7 DISTRIBUTIVE JUSTICE

The ethic of conservation is not always defined. In general, the production functions must be concave and not just quasi-concave, unless there happens to be a very high degree of substitution between goods. In the case of concave production functions, where there are no economies of scale, and large numbers of consumers, consumer conservation requires the competitive equilibrium where producers maximize profits and consumers maximize utility subject to a budget constraint.* In the case of increasing returns to scale there may be no production and distribution which is consumer efficient, even with the relevant concavity assumptions. The case is not presented for constant returns to scale and competitive equilibrium since the systems below are not competitive, but rather they exploit one class or another. Nevertheless, it is well to know that in this case the competitive equilibrium is the standard of measurement of welfare.

To see why quasi-concavity of utility does not assure the existence of consumer conservative allocations, consider a three person, three good economy. Let consumers I like goods 2 and 3, and be indifferent between the proportions consumed of each. Similarly, let consumer 2 like 3 and 1 and consumer 3 like 1 and 2. Let the commodities be produced from a single factor by identical production functions, f with increasing returns to scale, and let each consumer have an initial endowment of the factor, x. Then coalition $\{i, j\}$ will produce only commodity k, $i \neq j$, $k \neq i$, $k \neq j$. For the case of equal division of production, the coalition $\{1, 2, 3\}$ must assure each party at least $1/2f(2x)$ of j, since otherwise the consumer not liking j can

---

* Debreu and Scarf, "A Limit Theorem on the Case of an Economy," *International Economic Review*, 4, (1963).

entice one of the others to join with him. Of course, it is impossible to produce $f(2x)$ of i and $(1/2)f(2x)$ of j. Reducing the scale of output in good i will reduce the ratio of output to input in good i without bringing the input-output ratio in good j to an acceptable level. Of course, the scale of output of j cannot be increased without violating one person's benefit required to keep him from bidding away another from the arrangement. Formally, for increasing returns to scale, one cannot simultaneously solve

$$f(tx) + f((1 - t)x) \geq \tfrac{3}{2}f(2x)$$

$$f(tx) \geq \tfrac{1}{2}f(2x), \quad \text{and}$$

$$f((1 - t)x) \geq \tfrac{1}{2}f(2x).$$

To remedy this, it is possible to produce one of the goods at the level $f(3x)$, the one to be so produced to be determined by a random device. However, this would be unacceptable if there is (sufficient), risk aversion on the part of the consumer.

A possible way out is for each person to regard coalitions as being assigned probabilities of formation. In this way, they apply the rule, should i make an offer to j to leave the coalition $\{1, 2, 3\}$ it is quite likely that k will do so also. Then, the payoffs for coalition $(1, 2)$, $(2, 3)$ and $(3, 1)$ would be greatly reduced in threat against $(1, 2, 3)$. With only slight risk aversion, a possible solution might be one third probabilities of each of three alternatives which were relatively unfavorable to each of the three parties. With strong risk aversion an alternative might be equal quantities of goods to all three parties. Whatever solution was adopted, it could always be blocked by some coalition of two. Without application of the catergorical imperative, the resolution of conflict would seem impossible.

Evidently, social organization in which tastes differ are subject to more pressures under increasing returns to scale, *ceteris paribus.**

8 SOCIO-ECONOMIC EQUILIBRIUM

It is possible to combine the economic system with the sociopolitical regime. Without discussing the exact nature of sociopolitical relationships, it is assumed that these can be described by a convex and compact (closed and

---

* For the case where commodities are highly substitutable, see Shapley, "Nature on N-Person Game, VII, Cores of Convex Games," Rand Corp. memorandum, RM-4571-Pa Santa Monica, California and Scarf, "Notes on the Core of a Productive Economy," mimeographed, 1967.

bounded) set, denoted X. An element of x might have components for such things as political power or the holdings of various goods (perhaps for military use). For the economic, or more properly, the competitive aspect of the economy, there is a space of prices for various goods. In many cases, the set of prices includes any system of prices which are not all zero. Consider only the set of prices, $p = (p_1, p_2, ..., p_n)$, $p_i \neq 0$ for some i, and $\Sigma p_i^2 = 1$. This price space is in fact the unit sphere, S^{n-1}, in Euclidean n space. Now, given p and x, a competitive consumer i chooses demands or supplies of goods according to an *excess demand* correspondence, $E^i(p, x)$, where negative components refer to supply and positive coordinate to demand. It is required that the value of the excess demand be zero, i.e. the value of that purchased must equal the value of that sold. This condition can be written

$$pE^i(p, x) = 0.$$

The community excess demand correspondence is

$$E(p, x) = \sum_i E^i(p, x).$$

Evidently,

$$pE(p, x) = \Sigma pE^i(p, x) = 0.$$

Competitive equilibrium occurs whenever $0 \varepsilon E(p, x)$, i.e. whenever supply equals demand is possible. Also, consumers and others choose socio-political vectors in a correspondence, $F(p, x)$. A *general equilibrium* (p, x), is a pair in $S^{n-1} \times X$ such that

1) there is competitive equilibrium: $0 \varepsilon E(\bar{p}, \bar{x})$
2) there is *social equilibrium*: $\bar{x} \varepsilon F(\bar{p}, \bar{x})$.

The second requirement says that the socio-political state need not change from its present situation.

Example of socio-political forces to be incorporated in subsequent chapters are

1) demographic change resulting from level of consumption,
2) monopoly power exercized because one person or institution is powerful enough not to take the price system as given,
3) changes in wealth due to expropriation by groups with military power.
4) changes in demand or supply due to restriction of trade imposed by authorities.

In each case, there will be variables describing the basis for events or decisions and which in turn will be changed by events or division. These are the variables gathered under the auspices of the symbol, x.

In analyzing a particular socio-economic system, it is necessary to have a criterion for the existence of general equilibrium.

13   THEOREM

If

1) $E(p, x)$, $F(p, x)$ *defined on* $S^{n-1} \times X$, *respectively, are convex sets and upper semi-continuous*
2) X *is compact and convex,*
3) $pE(p, x) = 0$, *and*
4) *there is an i for which* $E_i(0, p_{\sim i}, x) > 0$ *for all* $p_{\sim i}, x$, *if* $p_i = 0$,

then there is an $(\bar{p}, \bar{x})$ *in* $S^n \times X$ *such that*

$$\text{(a)}\quad 0\varepsilon E(\bar{p}, \bar{x})$$

$$\text{(b)}\quad \bar{x}\varepsilon F(\bar{p}, \bar{x})$$

$$\text{(c)}\quad p_i \neq 0$$

Condition 4) will be satisfied if the ith good is in great demand when it is free. Usually, $p_i > 0$.

Proof   Evidently,

$$-e_i = (0, \ldots, 0, -e, 0, \ldots), e > 0$$

is never taken by $E(p, x)$ since otherwise

$$pe = -pe_i = p_i e = 0$$

whereupon $p_i = 0$ and $0 > -e = E_i(p, x)$ which is a contradiction of (4). It is easy to see that there is a convex, cone like neighborhood, N, containing e in its interior, the origin, and all positive scalar multiples of its points, such that y in N is not in $E(p, x)$. (Use the fact that E is upper semi-continuous a ndhence it maps the compact sets $S^{n-1} \times X$ onto a compact set).

Let $P = S^{n-1} \sim N$ (the set of points in S^{n-1} but not in N). Let π identify e in $E(p, x)$ with ke if ke is in P, $k > 0$, and with all of P, otherwise. π is a projection of $E(p, x)$ onto P, whenever possible. Then πE is upper semi-continuous as an upper semi-continuous correspondence (on a compact space) of an upper semi-continuous correspondence. Also, for given (p, x) $\pi E(p, x)$ can be shown to be mapped $1 - 1$ and continuously onto a compact, convex set. It is said that $\pi E(p, x)$ is a topological convex set. Consider the compound mapping

$$\frac{P \times X}{\pi E \downarrow F}$$
$$P \times X$$

Evidently, a compact topological convex set, $P \times X$, is mapped by an upper semi-continuous correspondence with topological convex ($\pi E(p, x)$, $F(p, x)$). Kakutani's theorem applies:* there is a fixed point, $(\bar{p}, \bar{x}) \varepsilon$ ($\pi E(\bar{p}, \bar{x})$, $F(\bar{p}, \bar{x})$). For $\bar{e} \varepsilon \pi E(p, x)$, either $k\bar{e} = \bar{p}$, or $0 \varepsilon E(\bar{p}, \bar{x})$. In the former case, $0 \geq \bar{p}\bar{e} = k\bar{e}\bar{e} > 0$ which is a contradiction. Hence, $0 \varepsilon E(\bar{p}, \bar{x})$. Of course $\bar{x} \varepsilon F(\bar{p}, \bar{x})$.

q.e.d.

The upper semi-continuity of E and F are not trivial to verify. It is helpful to know the following:

14 LEMMA

Maximization of a continuous function on continuous correspondences into a compact set yields maximizers which are upper semi-continuous.

9   CONSUMER CHOICE OVER TIME

Having justified the coexistence of competitive choice and other kinds of socio-political behavior, it is appropriate to return to economic theory. Until now, a major issue with regard to time has been neglected. Is the consumer's horizon finite or infinite; or less strongly, are there consumers with inifinite horizons? For example, does the theory of resource allocation for consumers apply whenever one or more consumers have an infinite sequence of consumptions, $(x^1, x^2, ...)$? What might the utility function of such a consumer be? As it happens, the resolution of this question is of some importance in finding the asymptotic properties of socio-economic systems.

Let xRy read x is at least as good as y. Preferences are *time separable* if

$$(x^1, x^2, ..., x^t, x^{t+1}, ..., x^s, x^{s+1}, ...)$$

$$R(x^1, x^2, ..., x^t, \bar{x}^{t+1}, ..., \bar{x}^s, x^{s+1}, ...)$$

---

* Kakutani, "A Generalization of Brower's Fixed Point Theorem," *Duke Mathematical Journal*, 8, 457–459, 1941.

if and only if

$$(\bar{x}^1, \bar{x}^2, ..., \bar{x}^t, x^{t+1}, ..., x^s, \bar{x}^{s+1}, ...)$$
$$R(\bar{x}^1, \bar{x}^2, ..., \bar{x}^t, \bar{x}^{t+1}, ..., \bar{x}^s, \bar{x}^{s+1}, ...).$$

In words, preferences are time separable if changing consumptions in two times has the same effect on preference no matter what are the consumptions at other times. More generally, preferences are *T-time separable*, if any change in consumptions T or more periods away has the same effect on preferences no matter what the consumption at other times. *T*-time separability allows memory and anticipation to influence preferences now, but the memory must be limited to T periods ago and the anticipation to T periods from now.

Preferences are *T-stationary* if there is a vector

$$(x^1, x^2, ..., x^{T-1})$$

such that

$$(y^1, ..., y^t, x^1, x^2, ..., x^{T-1}, y^{t+T}, ...)$$
$$R(y^1, ..., y^t, x^1, x^2, ..., x^{T-1}, \bar{y}^{t+T}, ...)$$

if and only if

$$(y^{t+T}, ...) R(\bar{y}^{t+T}, ...).$$

Ceteris paribus memory of $(x^1, x^2, ... x^{T-1})$ determines preferences.

Let

$$^sx^t = (x^s, x^{s+1}, ..., x^t).$$

Under sufficient continuity conditions, it can be shown that T-time separable and T-stationary preferences can be represented in the form

$$u = \sum_{t=0}^{\infty} u\left(^{t-T+1}x^t\right) \alpha^t$$
$$T = \sum_{t \leq T-1} u(^1y^t, ^0x^{t+T-1}) \alpha^{T-1-t}.*$$

This utility function is referred to as a *Koopmans* utility function. It is worth enumerating without proof the conditions sufficient to give the Koopmans utility function. A utility function, *u*, *represents* preferences if $u(x) \geq u(y)$ if and only if xRy: Preferences are *continuous* if x preferred to y implies $\bar{x}$ is preferred to y whenever $\bar{x}$ is near y and x is preferred to $\bar{y}$ whenever $\bar{y}$ is near y.

---

* Koopmans, T. C., "Structure of Preference Over Time," Cowles Foundation Discussion Paper, 1966, and Rader, *Theory of Micro-Economics*, Chapter 6, theorem 12, forthcoming Academic Press.

15 THEOREM

If

1) *preferences are T-time separable, T-stationary, and continuous*
2) $x^t(n) \to x^t$ *for all t and* $x = (x^0, x^1, ...)$ *is preferred to y but inferior to w implies that for large, n,* $x(n) = (x^0(n), x^1(n), ...)$ *is preferred to y but inferior to w, and*
3) *any pair of consumptions can be compared as to better worse, or indifferent and the comparison is consistent (i.e. xRy, yRz implies xRz),*

   then R can be represented by a Koopmans utility function with continuous u. If $R(x) = \{y|yRx\}$ *is always convex u will be quasiconcave.*

The u is continuous and quasi-concave, and α is positive and less than one. Intuitively, α represents the subjective rate of discount on future utility. Condition 2) of theorem 15 would seem to the point. For example, let $(x^0, \bar{x}^1, ...)$ be preferred to $(x^0, x^1, ...)$. Let

$$\bar{x}^t(n) = 0 \quad \text{if} \quad t > n$$

$$\bar{x}^t(n) = \bar{x}^t \quad \text{if} \quad t \leq n.$$

We must have for large n,

$$\bar{x}(n) = (\bar{x}^0(n), \bar{x}^1(n), ...)$$

$$= (\bar{x}^0, (n), \bar{x}^1(n), ..., \bar{x}^n(n), 0, ...)$$

is preferred to x. Evidently, high levels of consumption for a sufficiently long period of time can compensate for very low levels of consumption thereafter.

The arguments of the utility function may be in terms of per capita consumption and one component of the argument will be the rate of reproduction. Hence,

$$x^t = (c^t, 1^t)$$

where c^t is per capita consumption and 1^t is the ratio of consumer's family population in time $t + 1$ to that in time t. Under conditions of competition the consumer is constrained to prospective choices which satisfy

$$\Sigma p^t c^t N_t = \text{wealth}$$

where N_t is population size. The first order conditions for utility maximization can be shown to include

$$\frac{\dfrac{\partial U}{\partial x_i^s}}{p_i^s N_s} = \frac{\dfrac{\partial U}{\partial x_i^v}}{p_i^v N_v} = \frac{\sum_{s-T+1 \leq t \leq s+T-1} \alpha^t \, \partial u(^{t-T+1}x^{t+T-1})/\partial x_i^s}{p_i^s N_s}$$

$$= \frac{\sum_{v-T+1 \leq t \leq v+T-1} \alpha^{\,t} \, \partial u(^{t-T+1}x^{t+T-1})/\partial x_i^s}{p_i^s N_s}$$

or letting $h^s = \sum_{s-T+1 \leq t \leq s+T-1} \alpha^t \, \partial u/\partial x_i^s$,

$$\frac{\alpha^s h^s}{p_i^s N_s} = \frac{\alpha^v h_i^v}{p_i^v N_v}, \quad \text{or} \quad \frac{p_i^v}{p_i^s} = \frac{h_i^v N_s}{h^s N_v} \alpha^{v-s}.$$

Evidently, N_s and N_v are bounded as are h_i^v and h_i^s whenever x_i^s and x_i^v are bounded from zero and from infinity. If $h_i^s \neq 0$,

$$\frac{h_i^{v_k}}{h_i^s} \to c$$

for $v_k \to \infty$, and

$$\lim \frac{p_i^{v_k}}{p_i^s} \alpha^{s-v_k} = c \frac{N_s}{N}$$

where $N = \lim N_{v_k}$. If $c = 0$, $h_i^{v_k} \to 0$, which case will be considered below. For another, $\bar{\alpha}$, and $c \neq 0$,

$$\frac{N_s}{N} \frac{1}{N_i^s} \lim h_i^{v_k} = \lim \frac{p_i^{v_k}}{p_i^s} \bar{\alpha}^{s-vk} = \begin{cases} 0 & \text{if} \quad \bar{\alpha} > \alpha \\ \infty & \text{if} \quad \bar{\alpha} < \alpha. \end{cases}$$

By concavity of u, $\partial u/\partial x_i^t$ is non-increasing and by monotonicity it is non-negative. Hence $h_i \to 0$ only if

(1) $x_i^{v_k} \to \infty$,   or

(2) u is constant after a certain high value of x_i.

Case 1) is voided by virtue of a bounded $x_i^{v_k}$. Case 2) is voided by virtue of the fact that with $\bar{\alpha} > \alpha$, one could attain an infinite utility by waiting sufficiently long. Evidently, $\bar{\alpha} > \alpha$ is impossible. If $h_i^{v_k} \to \infty$, then $x_i^{v_k} \to 0$ for concave functions. Note that if

$$\frac{\partial U}{\partial x_i^{v_k}} \neq \infty$$

at $x_i^{v_k} = 0$, then after a certain finite period, $x_i^{v_k} = 0$ so that derivatives do not exist.

This is a paradox: There is nothing which requires all to have the same α. Evidently, if a consumer has less than the maximum α, then $\lim x_i^{t_0} = 0$, i.e. his limiting consumption is zero.

16 THEOREM

Let there be competitive consumers with preferences as in theorem 15 and continuous concave utility. In a limiting

$$((^{t-T+1}x^{t+T-1}), N_t)$$

(enumerated family by family), all except possibly the one consumer with largest α has zero consumptions of each good.

Limiting per capita consumption occur if less intense reproduction are preferable near the zero consumption. These conclusions are remarkable. Fixing reproduction, all except possibly the least myopic is reduced to the subsistence or slave level. Even if the poor have numerical superiority due to a faster reproduction rate, they are ultimately in a very bad state of affairs.

Varying reproduction along Malthusian lines leads to the numerical dominance by the most myopic (and least self sacrificing) type consumer, who may nonetheless be at a level near serfdom, depending upon how severe the myopia is. All these results are independent of the productivity of the consumers. In effect, high productivity will allow myopic consumers to consume large amounts at early periods, but they will ultimately indebt themselves to the least myopic. One is reminded of the frequent experience of many societies where interest rates are high and wealth is ultimately concentrated in the hands of the few whereas debt and obligations are concentrated in the hands of many.

Theorem 16 illustrates the general principle that the competitive system is exactly as good as its members, no better. It also calls into question the justice of the use of the Koopmans utility function and thereby of the justice of the use of the Koopmans utility function and thereby of the justice of complete, continuous references. Such results as above are avoided by the Protestant ethic whereby sustainable consumption paths are preferred. (In this way, the analysis supports the mother's view in *Look Homeward Angel*). One should not interpret too quickly the maxim "the purpose of production is consumption." Alternatively, in the absence of a Protestant ethic it may be necessary to institute consumption preserving programs such as public education and social security.

Proof For non-competitive societies, trade efficiency implies that consumers choose as if by a competitive price system.

The case of continuously differentiable u has already been taken. For a non-differentiable u, one can approximate by differentiable $u^n(x(t))$. In the limit, for some $n_k \to \infty$, $p^{nk}(t) \to p(t)$. There will be utility maximization with respect to the limiting price system at least in the components in which the chosen consumptions are strictly positive.

q.e.d.

For non-competitive societies, trade efficiency implies that consumer choice is as if it were competitive.

17 COROLLARY

If the consumptions are trade efficient with consumers having T-time separable preferences and continuous quasi-concave utility, then in the limit all except possibly one consumer has zero consumption of each good.

10 AN EXAMPLE: LAND OWNERSHIP IN A PEASANT ECONOMY

As an example of theorem 16 consider the case of two peasants living along side each other and consuming the products of the land. Let total land be L and let peasant 1 own $L_1(1)$ and peasant 2, $L_2(1)$. $L_1(1) + L_2(1) = L$, where $L_i(1)$ refer to land holdings in the first generation. Now suppose that peasant 1 has utility,

$$u^1 = \tfrac{1}{2}(L_1(1)^{\frac{1}{2}}) + u(\tfrac{1}{2})^2,$$

where u is the utility of his son. If the son has the same attitude to his son, and so on, then

$$u^1 = \sum_{t=1}^{\infty} (\tfrac{1}{2})^t (L_1(t))^{\frac{1}{2}}.$$

In the same way let

$$u^2 = \tfrac{1}{4}(L_2(1))^{\frac{1}{2}} + v(\tfrac{1}{4})^2,$$ where v is the utility of 2's son, or

$$u^2 = \sum (\tfrac{1}{4})^t (L_2(t))^{\frac{1}{2}}.$$

Denote the land rent at time t by $p(t)$. The trade efficient solutions are such that (marginal utility/rent) is equalized over different time periods:

$$\frac{\dfrac{\partial u^1}{\partial L_1(1)}}{p(1)} = \frac{\dfrac{\partial u^1}{\partial L_1(t)}}{p(t)},$$

$$\frac{\dfrac{\partial u^2}{\partial L_2(1)}}{p(1)} = \frac{\dfrac{\partial u^2}{\partial L_2(t)}}{p(t)}.$$

Without loss of generality, set $p(1) = 1$. Then

$$(\tfrac{1}{2})^2\, L_1(1)^{-\frac{1}{2}} = (1)^{t+1} L_1(t)^{-\frac{1}{2}}/p(t),$$

$$\tfrac{1}{2}\,\tfrac{1}{4}L_2(1)^{-\frac{1}{2}} = (1)^t\,\tfrac{1}{4}L_2(t)^{-\frac{1}{2}}/p(t).$$

Solving for $L_1(t)$ and $L_2(t)$,

$$L_1(t) = L_1(1)\,(\tfrac{1}{4})^{t-1}/p(t)^2,$$

$$L_2(t) = L_2(1)\,(\tfrac{1}{8})^{t-1}/p(t)^2.$$

Also,

$$L_1(t) + L_2(t) = L$$

so that

$$p(t)^2 = \frac{L_1(1)\,(\tfrac{1}{4})^{t-1} + L_2(1)\,(\tfrac{1}{8})^{t-1}}{L}.$$

Substituting above,

$$L_1(t) = L_1(1)\,L/(L_1(1) + L_2(1)\,(\tfrac{1}{2})^{t-1}),$$

$$L_2(t) = L_2(1)\,L/(L_1(1)\,2^{t-1} + L_2(1)).$$

Hence, $L_1(t) \rightarrow L$,

$L_2(t) \rightarrow 0$,

whatever $L_1(1)$, $L_2(1)$. In words, at the beginning peasant 2 will rent land from 1 in order to enjoy early consumption. He will leave his decendents with the debt thereby incurred and their wealth will be reduced. Peasant 2 will let out the land and thereby obtain future claims on the land that the family of peasant 1 owns outright.

If both parties were changing their land holdings with regard to others, then

$$L_1(t) = L_1(1) L(t)/(L_1(1) + L_2(1) (\tfrac{1}{2})^{t-1})$$

$$L_2(t) = L_1(1) L(t)/(L_1(1) 2^{t-1} + L_2(1)),$$

where $L(t)$ is their combined holdings. In this case, at least

$$L_1(t)/L_2(t) \rightarrow \infty.$$

Of course, if $L(t)$ is bounded from zero and growing less than exponentially, the asumptotic result is the same as for the fixed land case. Peasant 1 eventually owns all the land.

In contrast to this example, were consumer 2 to adopt a Protestant ethic whereby whatever his personal tastes, he never left his son with less land than himself, then his descendents would not be led to a state of immiserization.

Important institutions enforcing the Protestant ethic are

1) compulsory education,
2) social security and medicare,
3) laws whereby debts apply only to the physical estate and not to the raw labor and human capital of descendents.

These simply reflect the preponderant opinion in northwest European societies that children should not be left worse off then their parents.

11 A PARADOX OF UNBALANCED GROWTH

Many socio-economic systems place barriers to capital accumulation in certain sectors as was true of West European feudalism. Whenever the restricted sectors provide raw materials for the unrestricted ones, severe limitations are placed upon growth of the others. As it happens, as capital accumulates in the leading sector, factors of production which are positively related to population (namely labor) must tend to zero. Hence, if urban areas are leading in capital accumulation, their percentage of total population must decrease.

Let there be q primary factors whose output is limited by available factors. Let there be p secondary sectors where output may tend to infinity as (some) factors accumulate to infinity. Each sector has a population N_i, and a rate of reproduction, $\dfrac{dN_i}{N_i} = n_i$. There is *population equilibrium* if

$$\Sigma n_i N_i = 0.$$

Evidently, all stationary states are in population equilibrium.

18 THEOREM

Suppose

1) *among any group reproduction rates tend to minus infinity whenever all goods consumed per capita tend to zero.*
2) *reproduction per capita is bounded from above by a biological maximum*
3) *all factors used in secondary sectors escept those limited by population can be accumulated from output. Given population, accumulation to arbitrarily high levels of some factors leads to arbitrarily high levels of output.*
4) *output in secondary sectors is limited by raw materials available from the output in primary sectors.*
5) *outputs in primary sectors may tend to infinity as population increases but, in lieu of other factors, only if per capita output in primary sectors tends to zero.*
6) *If per capita consumption in secondary sectors is bounded from zero so are per unit time per capita accumulations of all factors not bounded by the secondary sectors' population.*

Then in population equilibrium, population in secondary sectors tends to zero whenever non-population factors are bounded in the primary sectors. Primary sector population tends to a state of equilibrium not accounting for the secondary sector.*

The usual interpretation of a primary sector is agriculture whereas a secondary sector can be thought as urban. Hence, if the urban sector alone accumulates factors, urban population must tend to zero. Assumption 6) is to be interpreted as a form of the Protestant Ethic whereby families accumulate no matter how high consumption levels are or what the possible tradeoffs are between consumption and saving.

Proof Because of the upper bound upon population and the rate of reproduction, arbitrarily small (negative) rates of reproduction are in-

---

* A special case of the theorem appears in William Baumol, "Macroeconomics of Unbalanced Growth: The Anatomy of Urban Crisis," *American Economic Review*, 57 (1967), 415–426.

compatable with population equilibrium. Therefore, per capita consumptions cannot all tend to zero.

As secondary sectors accumulate capital, if their population does not tend to zero, output will tend to infinity 3). This makes requirements of infinite output upon the primary sectors which can be provided only if there are arbirtarily large factor inputs in primary sectors. In the case of the hypotheses of the theorem, this is accomplished only by greater population and per capita output in primary sectors falling to zero. Since output in secondary sectors is limited by that in primary sectors, total output per capita tends to zero. To see this let y^1 be total output from the primary sectors, y^2 from secondary sectors, N^1 be population in primary sectors, N^2 in secondary sectors. Then

$$\frac{y^1 + y^2}{N_1 + N_2} \leqq \frac{y^1 + y^2}{N_1} = \frac{y^1}{N_1} + \frac{y^2}{N_1},$$

$$\leqq \frac{y^1}{N_1} + k\frac{y^1}{N_1} = (1 + k)\frac{y^1}{N_1}$$

for some $k > 0$. Clearly, $y^1/N_1 \to 0$ and $y^1 + y^2/N_1 + N_2 \to 0$. Since consumptions and investments summed over families equal outputs summed over sectors, per capita consumptions must tend to minus infinity, which is impossible.

To conclude, output in secondary sectors must be bounded which is possible only if population there tends to zero.

                                                                    q.e.d.

19   REMARK

If primary population tends to zero and if all primary sector family per capita consumptions therefore tend to infinity, then in fact primary population must tend to some positive level. Otherwise, one might imagine some families reproducing at large negative rates to offset the positive rates of the rich. Hence, there are two possible limiting cases. There is a neo-Malthusian state, with most people at the *subsistence level* of consumption yielding zero rate of reproduction. There are other states with virtually zero population but with some consumers at virtual starvation levels of consumption while others enjoy wealth beyond the subsistence level. These latter cases do not appear in any applications in this book.

The conclusion of theorem 18 can be obtained with fewer assumptions applied to a stationary state.

20 REMARK

If in a stationary state any family accumulates at least a positive proportion (above the natural rate of deterioration) of its consumption, that family must have zero members.

Proof Non-zero accumulation violates stationarity so that no surviving families can accumulate.

q.e.d.

Nevertheless, theorem 18 is of great use in cases where a stationary state is not assured.

CHAPTER 2

THE CYCLE OF EMPIRE

---

1 INTRODUCTION

It will be argued that the European period was unique among feudal-like periods in the history of other continents. Nevertheless, it has some similarities to some other times in other places. Could it be that feudalism was part of a natural process common to early states of all civilized societies? Is there anything in the dynamics of empires which leads to their replacement by a feudal regime or anything in the dynamics of feudalism which leads to an empire system?

In order to answer such questions there must be some notion of what an "empire" consisted. The classical empire, such as that of Darius, was not merely an expanse of territory under a single ruler, such as the Holy Roman or British Empires. It was a society characterized by

1) a centralization of political power in the hands of a relatively few individuals.
2) a slave economy operated for the benefit of the few,
3) with both agricultural and urban labor forces serving the aristocracy,
4) dominance over large expanse of territory, whose aristocrats or mercantile elements pay tribute to the capital city.

This characterization is a simplification, especially for later (classical) empires such as that of the Romans. But for the moment it is an acceptable basis of discussion of the economic and political decisions which appeared in the ancient empires. In interpreting 2), income was paid to individuals

a) independently of their economic performance, and
b) in accordance with the interests of a small group of aristocrats.

Under such a definition, ancient Egypt and the Mesopotamian city states were prototypes of an ancient empire.* As the number of commodities

---

* Robert Reeve, "No Man's Coast: Ports of Trade in the Eastern Mediterranean," in *Trade and Market in the Early Empire*, Polanyi, Arensberg & Pearson, eds.

increased, some degree of trading took place, but the basically master-slave relationship dominated economic life in the Babylonian and Persian empires.* Later, the short lived Macedonian empire as well as the Roman empire had well developed markets, but retained a mixed society with a large empire economy existing side by side with the commercial economy. Trade and markets were well developed, especially in the Eastern Mediterranean, but large expanses of territory such as Egypt were subject to extensive Roman taxes.† In the time gaps between the Western empires, there were the non-empire economies of the Hittites and the Mediterranean trading states.‡ Similarly, in India there appeared powerful centralized city states, after which there was a long Aryan age of decentralized economic life. Next there was a Magadhan empire (and successors)§, to be followed by a new "feudalism" (650–1200 A.D.) and a consolidation of divided states under the Muslims. Thereafter, the English and French entered (18th century). It should be stated that the slave system was modified in the later empires so as to favor the aristocracy but not exclusively to serve them. This modified system survived in India to the time of the British rule.**

Subsequently China will be studied in detail. Its case is one of the more prolonged periods, both of (classical) empires and feudalism. There were at least two feudal periods (ostensibly called empires) between the two empires.

Evidently, there is a "cycle," and it is the purpose here to offer an explanation. The explanation is highly tentative and undoubtedly will undergo modification. In particular, the analysis of the feudal economy and the empire economy is technical and relatively rigorous whereas the analysis of their interrelationship is less satisfactory from a formal viewpoint.

As the analysis proceeds, it will be seen that technological progress, both economic and military, plays a key role in the maintenance and decline of both imperial and feudal-like societies.

---

* See articles by Pearson, Polanyi, Oppenheim and Reeve, in Polanyi, Arensberg & Pearson, *op. cit.*
† Polanyi, "Aristotle Discovers the Economy," in Polanyi, Arensberg, & Pearson, *op. cit.* and A. C. Johnson, *Egypt and the Roman Empire*, University of Michigan Press, 1951.
‡ Reeve, *op. cit.*
§ D. D. Kosambi, *Ancient India*, Pantheon (New York), 1965.
** Walter Neale, "Reciprocracy and Redistribution in the Indian Village," in Polanyi, Arensberg & Pearson, *op. cit.*

2 IS SLAVERY EFFICIENT?

In the popular conception, slavery is effected by violence alone. Slaves are acquired in some campaign of conquest. It is commonly recognized that some people sell themselves into slavery but this is thought to be the exception. Certainly, this view seems to accord with Western experience in the last two thousand years. Nevertheless, it is quite possible for a whole population to voluntarily descend into slavery. This is the essence of theorem 16 of chapter 1, where in the long run, slavery is predicted for a trade efficient economy whose consumer preferences are continuous, complete, time separable and time invariant.

There are many historical precedents for the immiserization of the masses. Not all of these lead to complete servitude, but many come very close to doing so. Perhaps in the other cases, as in theorem 16 of chapter 1, it is just a matter of time.

There is a strong tendency for the non-slave economy to be transformed into one more nearly resembling slavery. In comparison to a landless and semi-employed state, the legal right to buy and sell slaves and to divide families at will may improve the productivity and the purely economic position of the slaves although it most often reduces his social and psychological position. Hence, the line between poverty and slavery may gradually recede until they are the same. At best, it may stop short of allowing the peasants to be bought and sold. Even without a slave trade, onerous taxes on, plus "adequate" social welfare for peasants would be sufficient for 2) of the definition of the empire to hold, since the definition of slavery is simply to labor without reward for the work done. At least five Byzantium emperors redistributed land to the peasantry.* In each case, the emperor favored the peasant over the land lord in order to assure a larger flow of revenues to his office. The tendency to slavery was resisted by the Byzantine emperors mainly because their subject lords instead of themselves were to reap the benefits. Moreover, there were intermittent reversals in the state policy. The emperors were not in agreement over the relative value of putting the peasantry under the lords or imposing controls directly from the empire.† Finally, it is likely that the emperors of Byzantium were not

---

*   H. Gregoire, "The Amorians and Macedonians," in Hussey, ed., *The Cambridge Medieval History*, Volume IV, Part I, Cambridge, 1966.

†   H. Gregoire, *op. cit.* and H. St. L. B. Moss, "The foundation of the East Roman Empire, 330–717" in Bury ed., *The Cambridge Medieval History*, Vol., IV, Part I, pp. 1–41, Cambridge, 1966.

emperors entirely in the ancient tradition since they ruled over a Christian state and used their revenues for many projects for the public welfare, such as hospitals, monasteries, and orphanages would not seem to create many taxes to compensate for the expenditure. Like the state charities, the policy of protecting the peasantry may have been partially motivated by ethics rather than expediency.

It should also be mentioned that an independent peasantry will contribute an army superior to that composed of slaves. This fact was uppermost in the minds of the emperors instituting land reform. Perhaps, the emperors were foresighted enough to see that the principles of the empire applied too strictly ultimately lead to the decline of the empire, as shall be seen. The emperor may have doubled as historian and may have been sensitive to the facts of many other fallen empires.

The producer efficiency of an economy is assured if all factors are employed and marginal rates of substitution are equalized between different industries. For consumer efficiency, price equals marginal cost and a degree of similarity between consumer taste is required. In the case of concave production functions, consumer efficiency will be assured if the slave owners are maximizing profits given their land and capital. *Per se* the existence of slavery is not necessarily inefficient. Inefficiency would result only if the owner were constrained from some other arrangement which was to his advantage. For example, the reduction in productivity due to the institution of slavery would give the owner the incentive to sell. Only if sale was not allowed would inefficiency be possible.*

The question remains as to when involuntary servitude is a means for gain to the owner superior to taxation of an independent agent. It would seem that the efficiency of slavery would turn upon the costs of control. In a household, the slave can be easily observed but in the countryside, control must reside with a foreman or such. To be efficient, a large number of workers must labor at the same place. Whenever such concentration is not sufficiently productive relative to work of smaller groups, share cropping or wages by piece work would appear to be more desirable means of extracting payment. An obvious disadvantage of a tax system is the possibility of the producer hiding his output from the tax collector.

---

* Calculations by Bergstrom in "On the Existence and Optimality of Competitive Equilibrium for a Slave Economy," *Review of Economic Studies*, forthcoming, indicate that slavery in the American South was sufficiently profitable that slave owners had little or no incentive to sell the slaves their freedom.

Explicitly, the owner must choose the following:
1) number of supervisors per laborer,
2) share of output paid to worker
3) hourly wages paid to workers. (Rents paid to owner can be regarded as negative wages).

In some instances, the number of laborers will also be a variable, but more often they are limited by local considerations. The payoffs from the various choices depend upon technology. For example, plantation agriculture would be more conducive to slavery than small scale farming. Hence, certain kinds of crops and terrain would be associated with slavery. Byzantium and Italy would illustrate cases where technology favored slavery of one form or another. The latifundia system whereby labor was bound to the land and subject to the whim of landowners was adopted.* It had none of the worst features of ancient slavery while serving slavery's economic function.

Also, the competence of the laborers would be an important consideration. The higher the level of knowledge of agricultural technique, the more advantageous are schemes allowing the peasant to make his own decisions. As shall be argued, the level of agricultural technique was relatively low in the Mediterranean and the loosening of control on the peasants was less profitable than in North Europe.

3   THE SLAVE ECONOMY

The immediate gain (minus loss) of defense is the excess of inflow of slaves from the frontier over whatever losses may have occurred in the frontier wars. The problem of greatest concern to the empire's ruler is that of allocating population and consumption between the countryside, the cities, and the aristocracy. The aristocracy seeks to maximize the number of urban goods which it receives given conditions for population equilibrium, (considering the slave inflow). This assumes that the aristocracy maximizes a relatively long run advantage. The more remote from population equilibrium, the less plausible such behavior would be. It would appear that in well populated areas, population equilibrium would be quickly established. In underpopulated areas, it might be otherwise. Birth and maturation take a long time to effect population growth but death is sudden and population decline quick. Only in the long run are population and labor synonyms.

---

* Moss, *op. cit.*

Under a slave economy the aristocracy receives virtually all those goods which the cities actually manufacture. Assuming their share of agricultural output, aside from demands for raw materials, is a small part of the whole, the aristocrats seek to maximize urban output.

The agricultural output above raw material requirements is distributed between the urban and the rural labor force in several urban and rural locations. Define the *malnutrition* income or consumption to be the one where potential reproduction reaches its maximum and the *subsistence* wage to be the one where reproduction in the agricultural sectors is zero. Due to the greater incidence of disease in the cities, urban areas will have negative population change at the malnutrition wage.

1 REMARK

In a population with a majority in the countryside, rural income will not be below the subsistence wage since that would violate population equilibrium unless the inflow of slaves were sufficiently large.

2 REMARK

If production is inter industry and factor connected, rural and urban laborers are not paid more than the malnutrition income.

Proof Surplus goods could be used to sustain more rural population with a balancing urban population. This would yield more urban output from the extra raw materials produced by the countryside.

q.e.d.

A larger urban population yields a larger urban output. In deciding between consumption for urban and rural workers, the aristocrats will be led to maximize the size of the urban labor force.

3 REMARK

If output is inter industry and factor connected, the aristocrats will be led to equalize the rate of change of population with respect to consumption in all sectors having slavery. If there is slavery in the rural sectors, urban income will exceed rural income.

Proof Were the rates of change of population to consumption unequal between two sectors, one could increase total equilibrium population by allocating consumption from that sector with the larger rate to that with the smaller. This would give a positive growth of population which could be offset by increasing population elsewhere. By factor connectivity the added labor could be used somewhere to increase urban output.

By virtue of their higher death rate, urban workers must be given more than their rural counterparts in order to equalize the rates of change of population with respect to consumption. Hence, if there is urban slavery, urban slaves get more than rural slaves. Otherwise, the added consumption will at best encourage urban labor to produce more so that there is reason for giving urban labor more consumption than otherwise.

q.e.d.

Increases in urban population can be attained only by increasing the rate of growth of rural population.

For a more formal analysis, divide sectors into two groups, one rural and the other urban. Let f be the vector net agricultural output (assuming no material imports from luxury (equals urban) goods). Let g be the vector of urban goods net of urban intermediate products but not of rural ones. Let β_{ij} be the amount of the ith rural good used in the production of the jth urban good, either directly or indirectly in urban intermediate products; the matrix β is defined as

$$\beta = (\beta_{ij}).$$

Let ϱ be a diagonal matrix giving the percent of rural goods consumed in rural sectors; $I - \varrho$ gives the percent consumed in urban sectors. Let N_1 be the sum of agricultural consumption and N_2 that of urban consumption. Let f_{N1} and g_{N2} be the rates of change of net output with changes in rural and urban population distributed say equiproportional among the various sectors. If birth and death rates in urban sectors are all equal for the same income levels as are birth and death rates in rural sectors, then the same incomes will prevail in all the urban sectors and the same incomes will prevail in all the rural section.

Agricultural labor receives income

$$\frac{\varrho(f - \beta g)}{N_1}$$

whereas urban labor receives (virtually)

$$\frac{(I - \varrho)(f - \beta g)}{N_2}$$

Total growth in population is given by

$$\frac{dN}{dt} = n_1 \left(\frac{\varrho(f - \beta g)}{N_1} \right) N_1 + n_2 \left(\frac{(I - \varrho)(f - \beta g)}{N_2} \right) N_2 \tag{1}$$

Therefore, the aristocracy seeks to maximize N_2 subject to setting the right hand side of (1) equal to the net inflow of slaves, with independent variables N_1, N_2, and ϱ.

The derivative forms of (1) reads:

$$\frac{\partial N_2}{\partial N_1} = n_1 + \varrho n_1' \left[f_{N_1} - \frac{(f - \beta g)}{N_1} \right] + n_2' (I - \varrho) f_{N_1} \bigg/ - n_2 + n_2' (I - \varrho)$$

$$\times \left[\beta g_{N_2} - \frac{(f - \beta g)}{N_2} \right] + \frac{n_1' \varrho g_{N_2}}{N_1} {}^{*} \tag{2}$$

$$\frac{\partial N_2}{\partial \varrho} = (n_1' - n_2')(f - \beta g) \bigg/ - n_2 + n_2' (I - \varrho)$$

$$\times \left[\beta g_{N_2} - \frac{(f - \beta g)}{N_2} \right] + \frac{n_1' \varrho \beta g_{N_2}}{N_1} {}^{\dagger} \tag{3}$$

where n_i' is the row vector of partial derivatives of n_i with respect to its arguments.

The first order conditions for maximization are

$$\frac{\partial N_2}{\partial N_1} = 0,$$

and

$$\frac{\partial N_2}{\partial \varrho} = 0.$$

---

* Since $d_N/dt = 0$, we have

$$0 = N_1 n_1' \varrho \left(\frac{\left(f_{N_1} - \beta g_{N_2} \dfrac{\partial N_2}{\partial N_1} \right)}{N_1} - \frac{(f - \beta g)}{N_1^2} \right) + n_1$$

$$+ N_2 n_2' (I - \varrho) \left[\frac{f_{N_1} - \beta g_{N_2}}{N_2} \partial N_2 / \partial N_1 - \frac{f - \beta g}{N_2} \frac{1}{N_2} \frac{\partial N_2}{\partial N_1} \right] + n_2 \frac{\partial N_2}{\partial N_1}$$

† Since

$$0 = N_1 n_1' \left(\frac{f - \beta g}{N_1} \right) - n_1' \frac{\partial N_2}{\partial \varrho} \varrho \beta g_{N_2}$$

$$+ N_2 n_2' (I - \varrho) \left[-\frac{\beta g_{N_2}}{N_2} \frac{\partial N_2}{\partial \varrho} + \frac{f - \beta g}{N_2} \frac{1}{N_2} \frac{\partial N_2}{\partial \varrho} \right] + n_2 \frac{\partial N_2}{\partial \varrho} - n_2' (f - \beta g).$$

In effect, the aristocracy seeks to maximize N_2. Evaluating (3),

$$n_1' - n_2' = 0*$$ (3a)

which is remark 1. Evaluating (2),

$$n_1 + n_1' f_{N_1} - n_1' \varrho \frac{(f - \beta g)}{N_1} = 0,$$ (2a)

which implies the following.

4 REMARK
Rural labor will be expanded beyond the point where added output is equal to rural income,

$$f_{N_1} < \varrho \frac{f - \beta g}{N_1}.$$

4 THE TERRITORIAL LIMITS OF EMPIRES

A sa simplification, let there be a numerical measure of tribute, V. Possibly, there are some value ratios by which one form of tribute can be transformed into another.

Define *surplus* as those goods which are not consumed by the workers. Evidently, in an empire surplus will be exactly urban output. Only a fraction of this will accrue to the emperor and the rest will go to his cohorts, the aristocrats.

Within limits, increasing the land area of the empire increases the surplus flowing to the capital. Of course, the area of the empire would increase by the square power of the boundary, and the quantity of slaves inflow per unit of land normally would decrease. Nevertheless, the added land would yield more to the aristocracy than the loss of slave per unit of land, until transportation costs became dominant. This can be seen to be the case by considering that in the absence of both transportation costs and slave in-

---

* If

$n_1 = n - d \left[ce(f - g)/N_1 \right]^{-1}$, $n_2 = c_0 n_1 + m$, n and m constants. For f, g numbers $\frac{N_1}{c\varrho} = \frac{N_1}{c(1-\varrho)} \sqrt{c_0}$. For f, g vectors, $\left(\frac{N_2}{c\varrho (f - \beta g)} \right)^2 - c_0 \left(\frac{N_2}{c(I - \varrho)(f - \beta g)} \right)^2 = 0$; c might be interpreted as calories per unit good consumed.

flow, an infinite amount of land could be utilized to obtain an infinite quantity of urban goods.

In general, the limits of the size of an empire are set by the costs of expansion. These might be quite large because of the existence of opposing power on the frontier or because of natural barriers which increase transportation costs. Also, the value of the land might decline to zero due to natural conditions such as sub-zero climate in the North, (Scandinavia or Mongolia), lack of precipitation (the Sahara), or the existence of a dense forest (Germany or the Congo Valley). For example, the extent of the Roman empire was limited by the desert to the South, the Germans and the forest to the North, the sea to the West, and the early Parthian "empire" to the East. Another limit on expansion might be due to the fact that the cost of transportation and administration from the frontier to the capital exceeds the proceeds from the land. In the Roman empire, lands on the sea were accessible from Rome due to Rome's facility at shipping. For lands distant from Rome and not bounding the sea, costs of transportation to Rome were high. This might explain why Hadrian did not attempt to solidify his control over the Mesopotamian area.* Any sub-region of the world can be dominated by capitals depending upon costs and returns between various capitals and regions. Clearly, a region in dispute will accrue to the empire which is willing to devote more resources to its conquest. One might think that a country would be willing to devote only those resources to conquest which could be repaid from domination. The prospective return represents the minimum resources which an empire would be willing to commit to a particular region. On the other hand, the empire may gain by threatening to commit resources in excess of this in the hope that by exceeding the resources another party might offer, the empire can dominate without conflict and without actually using the resources. Between these extreme strategies there is the possibility that the empire chooses an intermediat eposition of threatening with a probability greater than zero and less than one of employing resources sufficient to defend or conquer a region, even if this amount does not cover other prospective returns to that region. It would seem that a "rational" empire will employ the strategy of committing as many resources as are necessary to defend its territory, provided these are available. Certainly, this is upheld by the history of the Roman empire, where a standing army stood ready to defend relatively insignificant provinces against strong foreign encroachment.

---

* Gibbon, *The Decline and Fall of the Roman Empire*, I, p. 9 (Random House Modern Library, New York).

In addition there is a condition for internal stability of the empire. This requires that no combination of regions could break off and obtain a higher return than the empire. If such a grouping did exists, it would be motivated to revolt and the capital would be unable to expend the resources to return the region to its control. From the stability condition and the fact that transportation costs are positive, there would be no reason for the expansion of the empire beyond the locale, were it not that the capital is in command of resources which are not available to smaller sub-units, even acting in consort. Part of the resources might be due to superior military technology, but surely this would be a short-lived advantage. Indeed, were the empire's dominance entirely dependent upon the military factor, generals would be tempted to initiate the breakup of the empire and place themselves at the head of a new sub-empire. Therefore, the basis of the empire must rest upon some economic grounds such as the key location of a city *vis a vis* trade or minerals.

In particular, there are the gains of *pax Romana* which appear when wars between states are lessened. One should keep in mind that states who do not war must nonetheless be ever prepared for war since threats of retaliation require actual and not just potential resources. This itself should be regarded as an economic resource of large organization.

In general, it is by taking advantage of the diverse resources of different regions that an empire can obtain extra resources which a smaller region cannot provide. Of course, many of the advantages of conglomeration might accrue to a group of smaller regions practising free international trade. However, the smaller regions would be tempted to put up barriers to trade in hopes of collecting taxes and/or protecting home industries.

From the conditions of internal and external stability, there appears a position of territorial division and capital location which represents power equilibrium. This is the state of affairs which normally prevails among empires.

Let the expanse of an empire be denoted by X_i and its capital by y^i, $i = 1, 2, \ldots$. Evidently, the X_i are disjoint, and together they constitute the world. As any reading of ancient or modern history will verify, civil strife and external hostility are interrelated, the one aiding the other. What is required for a stable configuration of empires is that their areas of dominance be so constituted that the resources at their disposal be sufficient to ward off any threat from an alternative configuration,

$$\sum_i V_{X_i}(y_i) \geqq \sum_i V_{\bar{X}_i}(y_i) \tag{3}$$

for any other configuration ($\bar{X}_i$, $i = 1, 2, \ldots$). Alternatively,

$$\sum_i V_{X_i}(y_i)$$

must be maximum for all X_i whose union makes up the world. This is the principle of maximum value to tribute which has the corollary that for any empire, X_i,

$$V_{X_i}(y_i) \geqq \Sigma_j V_{A_j}(y_i) \tag{4}$$

for any disjoint regions, A_j, whose areas of dominance compose exactly X_i.* This is the condition for internal stability.

Let $X_i \sim A$ (read "X_i without A") be the empire, X_i with A excluded, and $X_i \bigcup A$ be the empire, X_i with A included, A condition for external stability also follows in that for any region A, not in X_i,

$$\sum_{k \neq i} V_{X_k} \sim A(y_k) + V_{X_i \cup A}(y_i) \leqq \sum_{k \neq i} V_{X_k}(y_k) + V_{X_i}(y_i). \tag{5}$$

If A is contained by X_j alone, then

$$V_{X_j \sim A}(y_j) + V_{X_i \cup A}(y_i) \leqq V_{X_j}(y_j) + V_{X_i}(y_i) \tag{5a}$$

which is to say that the resources available to the new power group, $X_j \sim A$ and $X_i \bigcup A$, are less than those available to X_j and X_i. Any attempt by i to annex A would be in vain since a revolution in X_i would leave A to be broken off again and rejoined to X_j. This coalition would exceed the available resources of $X_i \bigcup A$ and $X_j \sim A$, and certainly that of $X_i \bigcup A$. This point can be seen more clearly in the case where $A = X_j$. The union of X_i and X_j is not stable since a division can mobilize more resources. Also, by varying capitals, it is seen that (3) gives

$$V_{X_i}(y_i) \geqq V_{X_i}(\bar{y}_i) \tag{6}$$

for any other capital $\bar{y}_i$. Therefore (3) is seen to be necessary for world *power equilibrium*.

5 THEOREM

For world power equilibrium world tribute must be at a maximum with regard to the location of the capital of the empire and with regard to territorial division.

---

* Since

$$\sum_{k \neq i} V_{X_k}(y_k) + V_{X_i}(y_i) \geqq \sum_{k \neq i} V_{X_k}(y_k) + \sum_j V_{A_j}(y_j).$$

At the same time, it is clear that condition (3) is not sufficient for stable political equilibrium since in the situation where

$$V_{x_i}(y_i) > V_{x_j}(y_j),$$

$$V_{x_i \cup x_j}(y_i) > V_{x_i}(y_i),$$

there is a great temptation for empire i to expand and absorb j. The empire will avoid the fatal annexation only if it is foresighted enough to see that the union is itself unstable. However, after conquest and redivision, this should be brought home to the conquering nation. Hence, time and experience may be required to enforce power equilibrium.

Given that all aspects of an empire economy exist, what determines the extent of a particular empire? Normally, one would expect the political division to satisfy the conditions of political stability. When satisfied throughout the world, these conditions lead to power equilibrium. Possibly, several such equilibria exist and the particular one in existence depends upon historical developments. For example, if the world is the surface for a sphere, each point of which is exactly identical and if there is equilibrium, then all political units must be identical and therefore any rotation of boundaries, two poles fixed, delineates an equally valid power equilibrium.

A power equilibrium represents a stable political configuration provided there are no changes in returns to conquest. However, changes in production or military techniques may lead to radical changes in the benefits of domination or the costs of conquest, respectively. These changes may have unexpected results since the process of equilibration may be circuitous. For example, the arrival of Alexander's army in India led to the decimation of many of the western tribes, due to the superiority of the long Macedonian lance over the Indian chariot. However, India was too far from Macedonia to be profitably added to Alexander's empire, and the Eastern portion of the empire could not hold India unaided. One result was that Eastern Indian tribes were aided in their attempt to establish hegemony over India. The developing Magadhan Empire was thereby strengthened.*

If the power equilibrium does not exist, then there would be a sequence of territorial divisions, each of which supersedes the other and which do not have any particular direction of convergence. There would be territorial instability of an extreme nature as one division defeated another, etc. One can prove that power equilibrium is possible and therefore that such instability does not occur.

---

* Kosambi, *op. cit.*

The condition of power equilibrium is to arrange boundaries so as to maximize tribute. First observe that tribute can be no less than that with no centralized empires,

$$\int_{x \varepsilon X} V_{\{x\}}(x)\, dx.$$

Therefore, it has a lower bound. On the other hand, consider the maximum tribute that can flow from x, under any circumstances whatever (say with x as a capital of a large empire). Denote this by m_x. Then tribute cannot exceed the sum of this maximum over all x,

$$\int_{x \varepsilon X} m_x\, dx.$$

Therefore total world tribute is bounded from above. There is a least upper bound for world tribute, V,

$$\int_{x \varepsilon X} V_{\{x\}}(x, x)\, dx \leqq V \leqq \int_{x \varepsilon X} m_x\, dx,$$

and it is to be shown that there is a territorial division of empire which has the tribute V. If such a division can be shown to exist, then there is at least one power equilibrium The proof can be completed by means of application of some notions from measure theory.

The measure of a set is its area.

6 THEOREM

If:

1) *Empires of measure zero yield tribute less than or equal to that which would occur under total decentralization.*
2) *There is some concentration of territory which allows the formation of an empire of larger than zero measure and yielding more tribute than a decentralized society,*
3) *The tribute function is continuous.*
   Then there is a power equilibrium.

Proof For a given n, arrange the $X_i(n)$ in order of measure. Consider that tribute on regions of measure zero (zero area) is negible. Therefore, consider empires, $X_i(n)$, $i = 1, \ldots$, for which

$$\sum_{i=1} V\, X_i(n)(x_i(n)) \to V.$$

(Such a sequence of empire distribution must exist since V is the least upper bound for world tribute). Then $(X_i(n), i = 1, \ldots, n)$ can be chosen that

$$\mu_i^{n_k} = \mu(X_i(n_k)) \underset{k \to \infty}{\to} \mu_1 > 0.$$

Otherwise, the maximum measure would tend to zero as n tends to infinity and $V_{x_i}(y_i)$ would tend to

$$\int_{x \varepsilon X} V(x)\, dx.$$

Similarly, for any i, n_k is obtained by taking subsequence of the n_k^{i-1} for which the measure converges to

$$\mu_i \geqq 0.$$

By using the property 2)

$$\sum_{i=1}^{\infty} \mu_i$$

is equal to the measure of X.

Otherwise, on a set of positive measure X_0,

$$\sum_{x_i \subset X_0} V_{x_i}(y^i)$$

would tend to

$$\int_{x \varepsilon X_0} V(x)\, dx$$

Also for sets of measure μ_i, there is a subsequence of $(X_i(n_k^i)$, $n_k = 1$, 2, ...) which converges to a set (except possibly for a set of measure zero).* Such a set is denoted X_i. Then X_i is chosen inductuvely as the subsequence of the subsequence for which $X_i(n_k^i)$ converges to the set X_i. Now the measure of X_i is μ_i and therefore the sets $(X_i, i = 1, ..., n)$ decompose the space except for a set of measure zero. Also, the intersection $X_i \cap X_j$ are sets of measure zero since they are contained in countable unions of sets of the form,

$$X_i(n_k^i) \cap X_j(n_k^i),$$

which are sets of measure zero. Also, continuity of the tribute function gives

$$\lim V_{x_i}(y_i) = V_{\lim x_i} (\lim y_i)$$

so that ΣV_{x_i} is equal to V. Therefore, $(X_i, i = 1, 2, ...)$ is a power equilibrium.

q.e.d.

From the construction of the proof of the existence of the power equilibrium, that equilibrium will be attained as a limit of distributions of imperial

---

* There is a countable number of measurable sets for which any other measurable set is the union, except for a set of measure zero (Halmos, *Measure Theory*, pp. 62–64). Apply the method of proof in theorem 7.1, Chapter 1, Whyburn, *Analytic Topology*.

power with ever increasing quantities of tribute. Several such empire combinations might be simultaneously approximated. If there is sufficient territorial differentiation to make the equilibrium unique, then the triumph of a sequence of ever more powerful groups of empires would lead to equilibrium.

7   REMARK

The power equilibrium, if unique, is stable.

Some general statements can be made about the effect of changed circumstances upon power equilibrium. Roughly speaking, the added expanse of an empire will give less and less in the ways of gains from international trade. Decreases in costs of transportation will be a factor for larger empires since it opens up the opportunity for larger tribute provided a larger expanse of territory is organized under one capital. Also, the spread of military technology may increase the pressures on the border, whereupon there are still larger gains in tribute from the defense of a larger territory. On the other hand, the spread of non-military technology may allow production at home of goods formerly imported from abroad. This will tend to undermine the basis of empire. Also, the possible savings from transportation costs will cause manufacturers to search for techniques of producing goods amenable to local conditions.

Even without new techniques, the accumulation of population and capital will bring markets to a level where economies of concentration and large scale are not the exclusive province of the capital. Hence, economic progress may well be characterized by a larger tribute accruing to smaller areas of control.

It is often the success of the empire which brings its fragmentation. For example, the Roman empire divided into East and West not because somehow transportation became more expensive or because the external threat was less intense. Quite the contrary, in these spheres, there was every reason to continue and expand the empire. Possibly what happened was that the East became steadily less economically dependent upon the West. Because of the peculiarity of Mediterranean geography, the boundary of the empire was not longer from the break off of the Western part and perhaps shorter. For example, the boundary of Gaul with Germany was longer than the boundary of Italy with Germany and Gaul. And the boundary of the empire without Italy was shorter still. It would seem to be little gain for the Easterners relative to the gain for the Barbarians who were without the goods produced in the South. Hence, maximization of tribute would dictate the breaking off of the West and its addition to the barbarian domain. Of course, the barbarians were not subjects of an empire. Nevertheless, they were quite willing to devote the resources necessary to effect the change. Possibly, the East could have combined with the West to hold them off, but the cost may not have been commensurate with the gain.

One would expect the provinces of the Eastern empire to remain relatively intact so long as population and wealth were relatively stationary. However, should piracy increase on the Mediterranean, the resultant increase in transportation costs would further divide the empire. Piracy increased both because of the barbarians and because of the Muslim empire which acquired land on the Mediterranean. Thereafter, there was a rapid sloughing off the provinces which were accessible only by sea or which by land were relatively far distant. Between 600 A.D. and 800 A.D., the Eastern Empire was greatly contracted. The Muslim empire itself should be regarded largely as an extension of the Persian empire. That power which allowed Heraclius to retake Syria and Egypt from the Persians were forever lost before the Muslims. Possibly the difficulty of transport in the Mediterranean was the decisive factor in attaching these provinces to the land oriented Caliphate. It is possible that conversion of the Arabs to Islam cheapened transportation through the desert. Although little is known of their relative ferocity before and during the Caliphate, at least one theory is that the suddenness of the Arabic conquests was prompted by the denial of their familiar activities of war and theft.

These interpretations cannot be accepted without stronger evidence. Nevertheless, they indicate explanations alternative to those accrediting the decline of empire to rotting from within, exhaustion of mines and soil, religious fervor, great conquerors, or wise emperors. Luck, wisdom or skill can give the empire to one or another aristocracy, but technology and geography will determine its extent and location.

5 THE BARBARIAN ECONOMY

In the absence of a city dominated empire, there are many forms of regional organization. For example, a confederation may be formed for purposes of defense and even to regulate the relations between tribes. A decentralized feudalistic overlord or king may have some direct powers over the citizenry, but according to a code specifying the division of power between different classes. A kingdom may have absolute power over its subjects. All these forms of political organization have in common the fact that

1) there must be permanent "national" administration even if it rudimentary, and
2) the financing of the administration proceeds by taxation rather than by direct control of production.

For such political arrangements, there is no well defined aristocracy which will greatly benefit by expansion. Conquest tends to be for spoil rather than permanent dominance. Therefore, there is between such political groups a permanent state of hostility, where the strong prey upon the weak. This leads to dimunition of the population independent of health considerations. In a sense, these wars of plunder are a disguised blessing since they allow a population to exist at a higher per capita income than otherwise would be the case. In the absence of the deaths in battle, population equilibrium must be obtained by malnutrition and disease. Furthermore, the Northern barbarian has the advantage of dying due to extreme climatic conditions which further increases the equilibrium income. Hence, there is the manificent barbarian, especially in the North, who excels his Southern compatriot in every physical way. Only his ignorance of war and manufacturing prevent him from decimating the imperial boundaries and driving the civilized world into such enclaves as might be provided behind mountains and seas.

Invasions and conquests may lead to permanent barbarism, as in the case of the Frankish kingdom in Roman Gaul, or to eventual evacuation as in the case of the Kingdom of Jerusalem in Palestine. Which outcome occurs depends not only upon the conditions of political equilibrium, but in turn upon the amount of surplus in feudal and other barbarian economies. With no surplus there is no empire. Hence, absence of urban life is the prehistoric fact underlining the barbarian love of personal or at least tribal liberty. Nevertheless, in conquest or development, the barbarians obtain goods from and dominance over urban units. These constitute a source of power.

The surplus available for war in a barbarian economy constitutes the whole resources at that economy's disposal aside from minimum requirements for food and other "necessities". These remaining resources for war are best measured by total urban output, provided account has been made for the relative war making abilities of the barbarian and imperial troops. In comparing imperial and barbarian strength, two factors are of interest. The total urban output of an empire is likely to exceed tribute available for war since the subdivisions of an empire will absorb a certain portion of output, unlike the case of a decentralized economy. On the other hand, the decentralized economy is subject to extreme territorial division and therefore is more easily subverted.

In computations of surplus, one must be willing to distinguish regions not only as to their economic resources, but also as to the method of economic organization. For countries under a feudal regime, the choice of the capital city is not important and the country can be regarded as divisible into virtually infinitesimal parts, which can be broken off with an appropriate stimulus. Alone, they are the victims of any empire which might wish to establish its dominance, according to the strategy of divide and conquer.

To meet this problem, barbarian economies form alliances and kingdoms which present empires with more nearly indivisible units. There develops in these larger units a feeling of similarity and the notion of the "folk": a brotherhood larger than the tribe, made up of people of similar language and tradition. These kingdoms are somewhat artificially constructed and are therefore easily fragmented. Nevertheless, so long as they exist, they form the main impediment to the imposition of slavery. Expecially when the attributes of a slave economy are known, the barbarians are united against the empires and they fight valiantly in the cause of (relative) freedom (e.g. Europe against the Moors).

Being a part of a different social system, all that is required of the barbarians is that their resources exceed the maximum tribute which some combination of empires could mass against the barbarian lands. With a comparable level of techniques, the barbarians normally enjoy a higher living standard, and in defense of the system they appear to be willing to use all the resources of society, whether owned by serfs, lords, or cities. Therefore, the level of technique sufficiently high to conquer the barbarian region must be very high.

On the other hand, the empires must have resources sufficient to penalize the barbarians in excess of the return they would receive from wars of plunder. There is imposed a minimum size constraint on the empires near the barbarian borders. Aside from these considerations, the remaining empires must satisfy the conditions of power equilibrium.

An explanation of the empire cycle now appears. As the empire and the barbarian meet, the barbarian gradually learns the civilized methods of war making. Only steady technical progress in military affairs can keep the empire a step ahead of the barbarian. On the other hand, as the barbarian learns to defend himself against imperial slave expeditions, the slave inflow falls, causing slave incomes at home to rise in order to preserve population equilibrium Nevertheless, even with no slaves at all, the soldiers of the empire are not likely to be as healthy as the barbarians. Some empires may recruit their soldiers from barbarian lands, but this hys the disadvantage of hastening the day when the barbarians can make war as skillfully as can the empire. Eventually, the barbarian is knowledgable enough to use this superior strength. Small armies of barbarians are able to conquer areas of relatively large population.* The empire passes over to plunder and perhaps some barbarian leaders set themselves up as rulers. The outside culture is imposed; the cities which were constructed on tribute disappear, and a "dark" age reigns. So long as the cost of conquest by nearby empires or by a given region is in excess of the tribute from empire, the barbarian economy remains intact. Only the advent of a technical improvement can give one region an advantage over another. When this finally occurs, that region spreads its domination, likely as not enslaves those who are conquered, and constructs a new capital city. There are available cities with substantial resources, which can be the basis of real economic surplus beyond a totally decentralized economy. The empire is reborn under new masters and the cycle begins again.

6 THE END OF THE CYCLE

There appear at least three ways to end the cycle. First, an empire may dispose of barbarian problems, whether by conquering the barbarians, by minimizing contact with them, or by having such a rapid increase in technology so as to be always a step ahead of them. These appear to the methods used by the second empires in China and India. Second, under a feudal regime, there may be a uniform distribution of technical progress so that changes in the balance of power are minimized. Due to the discreteness of technical progress, this appears possible only if there is either very rapid or no technical progress. Third, there may be developed new institutions to cope with the needs for population equilibrium and a high standard of living. In effect, through the development of social science, technology can be turned to the very problem of the empire cycle.

The last two methods were used by feudalism in Northwest Europe. Technical progress proceeded relatively quickly throughout the feudal period†. This was due partly to the monastic orders, partly to the formation

---

* Lopez, *The Birth of Europe*, chapter 2, 1967, M. Evans, New York.
† White, Lynn, "Technology and Invention in the Middle Ages," *Speculum*, XV, (2).

of an idea of progress. Even in early periods before rapid technical change, when the conquest of large territories formed kingdoms such as the Frankish "empire" of the Merovingians and Carolingians, the dislike of slavery inherent in Germanic culture and the Christian religion prevented the formation of an empire economy. Finally, the Roman Catholic Church emphasized celibacy and abstainance, which led to a moderation of the growth of population. For example, at one time, fully one third of the population of Spain was in monastic orders.* It became the habit, even in less Catholic countries, to postpone marriage until a minimum living standard could be insured for the family.† As time proceeded, a new era emerged in which the economy was neither imperial nor feudal, although France may have been returning to an empire economy under the Bourbons.

7 CAPITAL AND TECHNOLOGY:
WHY THE CYCLE STOPPED IN THE WEST INSTEAD OF CHINA

The above remarks are highly speculative. In order to justify them, some historical evidence is considered.

In the last four hundred years, the dominance of Western Europe over the rest of the world was assured by its technological lead. Technology became the instrument by which the cycle of empire was everywhere disturbed. Hence, technology deserves special consideration. Constrast with China is informative since China itself enjoyed rapid rates of technical change. There is some difference in family orientation which makes the Westerner more individualistic and more motivated toward personal success.‡ However, this does not explain why success should be oriented to technical or economic accomplishments. The Greeks and Romans were individualistic Westerners, but their efforts were more toward scholarly, artistic, and military success than toward material gain. An appropriate success motivation might amplify the rate of economic and technological growth; but it is not a sufficient explanation of that growth. It will be seen that the peculiar fabric of European institutions and historical forces together caused a quite different effect on Europe than on China.

---

* Russell, "Recent Advances in Medieval Demography," *Speculum*, XL January, 1965, pp. 84–101.
† Russell, "The Preplague Population of England, *Journal of British Studies*, (V) May 1966, pp. 1–21.
‡ Hsu's, F. L. K., "Cultural Factors" in H. F. Williams and J. A. Buttrick, eds., Economic Development: *Principles and Patterns* (New York, 1954).

If tradition is to be believed, 1500–1100 B.C. was a period of city states similar to the early Indus river valley and perhaps derived from the Indian example. From 1100 B.C. to 771 B.C. under the Chau dynasty, this state of affairs continued with considerable technolgical progress. From 771 B.C. to 256 B.C. still ostensible under the Chau dynasty, China fell into a decentralized state. Still behind the West, China did add some inventions, of her own, e.g. the crossbow. From 206 B.C. to 280 A.D., under the Ch'in and Han dynasties, there was a period of empire and China at last caught up with the West in technology. During the decentralized period 222 A.D. to 509 A.D. (the Six Dynasties), and the empire of Sui and T'ang from 589 A.D. to 907 A.D. China was far ahead of the West. Thereafter, it seems likely the population greatly increased but per capita income was more or less fixed or falling until Ghengis Khan. This period was characterized by a separation of empire in the South and in the North. There is superficial resemblance with Europe: Visigoth, Lombard and Frankish kingdoms in the West and the Byzantine empire in the East. However, the analogy is entirely superficial since nowhere in China did the central government lose control, as in the European West. The barbarians of China chose to preserve the traditional society and work through the traditional methods of administration. Hence, for present purposes, the empire persisted from 589 until the Republic in 1911, over 13 centuries. China had three empires and two periods of economic and political decentralization.

The West had a period of commercial and industrial expansion in the late Middle Ages which continued until the advent of modern times to become the longest period of relatively steadly economic development known up to that time. In contrast, while China was finally reunited under the Tan and Sung dynasties, after the 10th century, there was only an increase in population with no significant increase in the standard of living. Trade increased, but agriculture was not greatly improved. Why did the West accelerate its economic position, partly on the basis of an increase in technological knowledge, when China did not?

There are also some similarities. Neither in Europe nor China did the merchant have a high social status. After accumulating wealth he often purchased land and titles or bureaucratic position. Nevertheless, both areas went through a commercial revolution where there was a great expansion of trade. Indeed, Southern Europe offers a useful contrast to Northern Europe. In the South, economic progress was more nearly confined to trade and manufacturing whereas the North took the lead in agriculture. Since always the greater part of the population lived in agriculture, this difference proved to be decisive for the North. Hence, the prototype of European development should not be the Italian city states or the surrounding lati-fundia but the Northern manorial system. Once this is accepted, it becomes evident that technology was the basis of growth. First, the axe felled the forest. The heavy plow subjected it. Finally, the three field system gave it maximum output. The formulae of success was a technological one.

It should be clear that present concern is not the wide sweep of Chinese and Western culture, but rather the comparative level and dissemination of the industrial arts. These are defined to include only techniques which allow the production more quickly or more easily of clothing, food, means of transportation and communication, housing, and tools for defense, and which are accumulative in their nature. Excluding the division of labor as such a technique, each new process is dependent for its creation upon those which preceded it and upon the general intellectual position of the popula-tion, upon the diffusion of such arts and upon the attitude of the would-be innovators toward them.* In effect technology is an industry like any other in which there are interrelated production processes and increasing returns to scale. The returns increase very rapidly with scale and hence it is generally organized under the auspices of an institution controlled by the state. In analyzing changes in the level of technology, no distinction will be made as to whether new techniques arise from the culture itself or were instead intro-duced from some other culture. With these ideas in mind, relevant conside-rations are differences in communication between cultures, the dissemination of technology, the speed of technological change, and the source and nature of the wealth of the civilization. Hopefully, some conclusions can be drawn as to the explantion of the differences in technological change following the political and economic revivals.

Possible explanations of the differences in development of China and the West are

1) Western Europe had more contact with other civilizations (especially the Greco-Syrian culture).
2) Being spatially decentralized, Western Europe presented a more favorable atmosphere for heterogeneity and originality.
3) The grouping of technological inventions gave the West the idea of progress.

There are other theories of development although some such as the climatic theory are not relevant to the comparison.

---

* Clarence Ayres, *Theory of Economic Progress*, University of North Carolina Press, Chapel Hill, North Carolina.

The differences between China and the West were not due to differences in inter-cultural contacts. It is not absolutely essential to have a large volume of inter-cultural communication. However small a small as opposed to a large volume of contact will simply slow or increase the speed of the flow of techniques. But even such slow exchange could have been of less use to China than to the West, as China had the disadvantage in many cases of being first. Joseph Needham lists some 58 different innovations transmitted from China to the West in which the time lag was as great as eighteen centuries and rarely less than four.* It is apparent that China was far ahead of the West or even other civilizations in such war techniques as gun powder, artillery, the crossbow; such industrial techniques as silk-working machines, iron casting, deep drilling, the wheel-barrow, paper printing; architectural and building techniques; transportation techniques such as types of bridges, rigging rudders; agicultural techniques like breast-straps and horse collars; an extensive canal system controlled by gates; irrigation; compasses, etc. These time lags would not be so extreme with the Islamic, Indic, and Byzantine civilizations, but still the Western cultures really had little to offer China in the way of techniques during her periods of expansion at the beginning of the Christian era and during the 7th and 8th centuries. There are several possible exceptions such as the screw, crankshaft, and clock work, although for the last two, Needham argues Chinese precedence. Needham might be overstating the margin of China over the West. For example, R. J. Forbes claims that gunpowder was actually discovered in the West in the 13th century,† while Needham places it in China in the 8th century and cites 850, 919, 1100, 1200, and 1000 (A.D.) as dates for various uses of it.‡ At any rate it is clear that in mere volume of techniques China was first and certainly was in no position to use foreign techniques to the extent that the West did after the fall of the Roman empire.

Still, China might have adopted with great profit one foreign innovation, a phonetic alphabet from the West. Her use of the printing press and indeed the dissemination of knowledge through education were greatly limited by a difficult ideographic script and the lack of a convenient number system as provided by the Arabic numerals. The use of movable type, possible with a phonetic alphabet, would have allowed mass production of books and would have made literacy attainable by the mass of people. Only recently

---

* Needham, *Science and Civilization in China*, I (Cambridge, 1954).
† Forbes, *Man the Maker*, p. 118.
‡ Needham, *op. cit.*

have printing systems been developed to reproduce ideographs with ease. In such a case an odd reverse takes place, since some of the ideographic systems (e.g. Japanese) are actually easier to learn than phonetic alphabets.

However, even had she been more conversant with other civilizations, China's religious identification with her script, persisting until recently, would probably have prevented the adoption of a phonetic alphabet. Without efficient notation it is inconceivable that China could have participated in an industrial revolution on Western scale. Even so, there is no reason to suppose that she could not have sustained the same kind of world trade Spain and Portugal did or that technological and economic progress should have come to the halt that it did in the 12th or 13th century.

An elaborate scientific system such as the Greeks and Babylonians contributed to the West would not appear to be necessary for technological change until relatively late in the technological evolution. This is certainly borne out by the earlier history of China in which she far exceeded the Greeks in technological knowledge, with the aid of philosophies which, far from supposing some given order of the universe, denied any order at all. The Taoist held that nature was basically inconsistent and unpredictable while the Confucian held that custom and society were the only object worthy of concern and dedication.

China developed with a philosophy which deterred systematic science, the only Western import from which China could have benefited significantly.

There is no reason to suppose that education was more widespread in Europe than in China. The difficult script narrowed the literate elite in China during the five or six centuries of expansion, but beyond the rudiments of arithmetic and perhaps the ability to write one's name, the bulk of Europe remained uneducated. Most of the books of the West were written in Latin even into the 14th and 15th centuries. Perhaps the most significant development in general education was the widespread use of advanced accounting methods among the business classes of Italy and later North-western Europe, facilitated by the Arabic numerals but first dependent upon the rapid use of the abacas and the counting table.* This was quite helpful in stimulating trade, but it is doubtful that in China it would have been a decisive factor in spreading technology any more than it had been in the West.

---

* Sombart, "Medieval and Modern Commercial Enterprise" translated by Riemersma in *Enterprise and Secular Change*, eds., Lane & Riemersma, Irwin, 1953.

The isolation of China was not really the decisive factor in bringing her progress to a standstill, for China never really came to the point where a widespread and efficient knowledge of either reading or arithmetic (beyond the abacus) were essential to continued technological change. And further, she really did not need communication with other civilizations in industrial processes because so many of them had originated in China.

The great value of spreading technology is the placing before a large number of minds the real problems and the real alternatives in doing certain jobs or producing certain goods. Insofar as such dissemination aids technological progress, territorial division of labor is quite unfavorable to technological change. This is particularly true in earlier stages in which there were no systematic thought patterns effective either in solving technological problems or in innovating new processes to speed up production of old materials. At the same time, decentralization diminishes the size of endeavor, insofar as smaller equipment with less output is needed for small economic units. The decentralization is most advantageous when it can reap the benefits of the diffusion of techniques into every village and at the same time avoid the necessity of large scale organization and operation to implement such techniques.

While China suffered much less from the extreme feudalism of the European states, maintaining even during her "darkest" age the semblence of unity of economic regions and, periodically, of the whole country, Europe after the collapse of Roman authority made no pretense at continental unity and rarely at regional consolidation. Even as economic expansion accelerated, until the time of the discoveries in America, the European trading cities remained somewhat independent both of each other and of the productive activities of the agricultural communities with which they dealt. Thus, every village had its blacksmith, who was versed in all the metallurgical techniques of his day; and every peasant or serf grew his own wheat or turnips or millet, tended his own animals and kept his own tools.

Even as techniques were being disseminated into the villages, the guilds in the larger towns were building their own power in opposition to interchange of knowledge, desirous of hoarding their skills and protecting their positions. It is likely that this counter effect reduced significantly the spread of technical knowledge through the medieval world, but only late in the period.

It is at least possible that such dissemination gave the European some advantage over his Chinese fellow, but one must not press the point too hard lest he argue for reduced production through reduced specialization. The territorial division had definite advantages for the technological process, whether or not these exceeded the disadvantages of a smaller output.

One would expect that the psychology of the population would be important in technological development. In particular, the consciousness of the possibility of technological improvement and regard for it as a legitimate end are crucial. The elite in the Roman empire, and in the Greek city-states before it, exalted the philosophical, the artistic, and the theoretical to the detriment of the practical. On the other hand, for the clergy and especially the monks, manual labor and the practice of the industrial arts was not just an acceptable and desirable end but was a religious ceremony, so that Aquinas had to protest that there were types of productive labor other than physical work.* Even this, in the form of Taoism, the Chinese had had since at least the 4th century B.C., so that Taoists were ferever proclaiming the harmony of the universe, the Yin and the Yang, the light and the darkness, the male and the female as being the essence of every act and in particular the essence of such skills and crafts as medicine, handiwork, mechanics, dressing meats, etc. Nor could it be said that the superior European heritage of the Greek and Hebrew concepts of law were of much use until the 17th and 18th centuries development of modern science. Other differences between West Europe and China can be found. First, the West has an obvious detachment from any sentimental ties to ancient civilization or some glorious defunct past, in contrast with the Chinese turning ever backward to a sixth century B.C. age of classical harmony. More important, the newly-civilized barbarians had the advantage of seeing simultaneously commercial expansion aided by the reconquest of the Mediterranean by Europe and a rate of advance in the state of technology unparalleled in past history. It does not matter at all that most of these were brought in form the outside or that many were developed only upon receiving some vital tool for general progress from some other culture. What does matter is that the acquisition of new techniques was of such speed as to give some basis to the feeling of progress and to make the European receptive to the kinds of risks and adventures which he soon proved to be.

That the speed of technical change was a great as claimed can be seen from the list of techniques drawn up by Needham and quoted previously. From the 9th to the 14th centuries, and particularly in the last three centuries, nearly as many Chinese innovations were introduced into Europe as had been developed in the first eight centuries of China's expansion,

---

* Klemm, *A History of Western Technology*, p. 69.

from the 4th century B.C. to the 4th century A.D., or as in the six centuries of relative Chinese prosperity and progress from the 7th to the 12th century.* At the same time Europe was drawing heavily on the Muslim world for Arabic numerals, medicine, etc., and had already absorbed Roman culture from the Byzantines and the surviving Latins. Further, half as many again Chinese innovations were introduced into Europe in the 15th century. Finally, add to this the development of the crank shaft, as important a machine development as any since the Wheel, and the clock,† and one gets a picture to compare with the best era of Chinese inventions, with the rather slow progress of the Greeks and the Romans, with the five milleniums of the growth of Egyptian and Mesopotamian civilizations, and the countless ages in the evolution of Neolithic and Paleolithic cultures. Certainly no better circumstances had been previously presented for a theory of pregress, so important in later European advancement, scientific, technological, commercial, and territorial.

That such a theory of progress was imminent is evidenced by the writing of Roger Bacon in the 13th century when he predicted solutions to various human problems so that men would be seen flying as birds and riding in boats which went faster without oars than those with them, while a century later Leonardo de Vinci was busy drawing all kinds of "fantastic" machines allowing man to do unheard of things.‡ Perhaps this was the first time in the history of the world that men became aware not that there had been great progress in the future.

There are at least two ways in which a theory of progress hastens technical progress. First, capital invariably accompanies privilege. Should the upper class see the possibility of progress, they are more ready to invest in new ideas. Expecting rewards, they are willing to take risks and to wait. Second, some people will be excited by new prospects and devote their leisure to technical developments. The second factor was somewhat accentuated by the structure of medieval society.

One way or another, the upper classes sustain themselves upon the surplus produced by the economy, and because sustained technological progress is inconceivable without the participation of those who have the time the attitude the elite take toward technological growth is important.

---

* Needham, *op. cit.*
† Needham, *op. cit.*, and Usher, *A History of Mechanical Inventions*, McGraw-Hill, New York, 1929.
‡ Klem, *op. cit.*

While the fathers of the medieval church saw work as being their duty and technological knowledge as being the base of man's triumph over nature, the Chinese civil servant looked upon the society in which he lived, the state and its organization, as the foundation of human welfare. Augustine, one of the most mystical and unscientific medieval churchmen, wrote "In Praise of Creation" in the 5th century:

"What varieties has man found out in buildings, attires husbandry, navigation, sculpture, and imagery! What perfection has he shewn in the shows of theatres, in taming, killing, and catching the wild beasts! What millions of inventions has he against others, and for himself in poisons, arms, engines, stratagems, and the like! What thousands of medicines for the health, of meats for the throat, of verses for pleasure, of musical inventions and instruments. What excellent inventions are geography, arithmetic, astrology, and the rest."*

But the Chinese civil servant looked backward, not to the technical achievements of their ancestors, but rather to their art, their literature, their customs, and their organization and harmony. Thus among the scholars (who were for the most part the civil servants) the philosophy of 6th centry B.C. Confucious remained the ideal until the end of the 19th century. Its concern was for order, formality, the family, morality in personal relations, etc. Even the most scientific philosophers, the Taoists, spoke in terms of the harmony of the universe, and in reading Chinese philosophy, one cannot help but believe that harmony was the most admirable word in the language of a people whose civil servants often felt that "it's old" was sufficient defense for a policy.

Surely, the glory of China, its strength and prestige, has ever been its unity and stability. China itself was bound up not only by the continental state typical of all the ancient empires, but also by the Grand Canal, which ran from North to south and which was built and maintained only with the labor of millions of peasants, giving up their labor and their lives. Even more expensive in such terms was the Great Wall which protected China from northern invaders, valued it is said in millions of lives. All this was built at the prompting of a central administration and the Chinese could not help but be impressed by the necessity for great common sacrifice to attain future stability and prosperity.

The base of Chinese surplus was quite different from that of the West. China depended upon irrigation, canals and locks, state roads, walls,

---

* Klem, *op. cit.*

government support of agriculture, salt, copper and iron monopolies, etc. North Europe depended upon horse power (the Chinese peasant used the slower ox), with all the advantages due to the horse collar, the horse shoe, and the heavy plow; the water wheel and the windmill, the invention of the crank which transformed reciprocal motion into rotary motion, and the use of cast iron facilitated wider use of machine power. In particular, the textile industry was very important as the first general manufacturing enterprise of Europe, which was aided by the invention of the spinning wheel in the 13th century.

The surplus of the European Middle Ages, though cruder perhaps, stood primarily upon technology, and her elite was well aware of this, whereas the surplus of China was to be more attributed to mammouth public works built by mass labor, and to the division of labor, each being products of superior organization, not of the state of industrial arts. Lynn White noted: "From the twelfth and even from the the eleventh century, there was a rapid replacement of human by non-human energy wherever great quantities of power were needed or where the required motion was so simple and monotonous that a man could be replaced by a mechanism. The chief glory of the latter Middle Ages was not its cathedrals or its epics or its scholasticism: it was the building for the first time in history of a complex civilization which rested not on the backs of sweating slaves or coolies but primarily on non-human power.*

The Europeans believed in progress and saw the advantages of technical change in the production of goods. This explains more than anything else why gentlemen, scholars, and clergy began increasingly to devote themselves to the study of the experimental science.† Meanwhile their Eastern counterparts were still fighting philosophical battles over the harmonies of society and nature, battles which produced important results even for Western thought,‡ but which did not produce sustained technological progress.

The cycle of empire accumulates manufacturing techniques which thereby constitute an even larger body which the newly conquering barbarians

---

* White, "Technology and Invention in the Middle Ages," *Speculum*, Vol. XV, no.2, p. 156.

† Lynn Thorndike, "Magic, Witchcraft, Astrology, and Alchemy," ch. XXII Bury, *et al.*, ed., *The Cambridge Medieval History*, Vol. VIII, Cambridge University Press, Cambridge, England, 1936.

‡ Leibnitz apparently drew from Chinese philosophy; his mathematical formulation of logic was inspired by the chinese ideograph. See Needham, *Science and Civilization in China*, Vol. II, pp. 291–292, 340–345, 496–505.

discover all at once. There will be a tendency for them to inpute to this a theory of progress which will help end the cycle. But this effect will be limited if the barbarians simply allow the old civilized society to do it. Radical changes from empire to feudalism are more favorable to the development of the idea of progress and to its implementation. The tendency to a theory of progress will be still stronger when it is new areas such as Western Europe which are becoming civilized without direct reliance on older civilizations. Territorial divisions and economic decentralizations will contribute to the velocity of technical change and magnify the bunching of innovation. The work ethic of the Christian church further reinforces the preoccupation with technological progress. In contrast, an irrationalist philosophy may be detrimental to the construction of this idea of progress, but not so detrimental as will a general feeling that progress is due to a more effective utilization of given resources rather than an expansion of knowledge.

CHAPTER 3

FOUNDATIONS

1 GERMANIC TRADITION AND TECHNIQUES

The manorial system, surrounded by small farms, formed the economic core around which the social regime of feudalism was established. Evidently, the strictest form of the system predominated in France and West Germany.* The system was unique in Europe and indeed in the world. The major distinguishing features were:

1) a relatively self-sufficient regional economy, whose boundaries were limited by transportation costs and the nature of the market.
2) extensive economic obligation to the lords who served as the judicial and administrative government,
3) otherwise, a system of free individual agriculture, except that some labor was bound to the land,
4) a level of technique which was above that of the latifundia system which the manor replaced.†

2) is a distributional-political arrangement common to many societies under the pressure of recurrent invasions and warfare (e.g. China, Japan, Persia). Given the distribution of income and the disintegration of centralized political power, 1) naturally follows.Therefore, the distinguishing characteristics of European feudalism were 3) and 4). 4) was perhaps a part of the natural historical process. 3) represented a unique organization whose implications shall be explained. The characteristics included a definite assignment of land to individuals who were responsible for its cultivation and who were granted its produce after possible payment to the political authorities, or to a sharing partner, the lords. Labor services to the lords might be regarded as part payment. Normally, the land was intended to be the source of livelihood for those who tilled it, and the return was sufficient for wife and children. Whatever co-operation took place between individuals

---

† Bloch, M., *Feudal Society*, translation, University of Chicgo Press, 1961.
* White, L., *op. cit.*

was of a voluntary nature and proceeded according to established rules of exchange.* Thus defined, the system predominated in Northwest Europe perhaps in the period 1000 A.D. to 1350 A.D.

The Germanic tribes seem to have invaded the Roman lands every generation. Between 250 A.D. and the time of the Huns (365 A.D.) the Goths made war on the Romans in the Balkans perhaps every 40 years, while the western tribes made war still more often. Then at the end of the fourth century, the Goths (under Aleric) and the western tribes invaded more or less simultaneously. Thereafter, the invasions were more frequent and of longer duration.† Evidently, the Germans had a sufficient food supply for war. According to Bloch,‡ once the conquest of Rome was completed, the north became greatly depopulated. Evidently, over-population was not the source of the pressures on Rome from Germany, and is unlikely ever to be so, since there must be an adequate food supply to sustain the long marches through hostile territory characteristic of ancient war. Tacitus describes the Germans as participating in an agriculture which was individual even if primitive. Undoubtedly, the Germanic tribes enjoyed a relatively high level of agriculture, even before the introduction of the new techniques, due partly to their method of organization. In particular, they had a large store of cattle and pursued a form of agriculture now characteristic of a thinly populated region.§ Accounts by Latouche of the work of the Coulanges and subsequent German scholarship indicates that individual ownership and operation of farms was characteristic of pre-invasion German agriculture.** Latouche suggests that as early as the first conflicts with Rome, the Germans also had superior techniques in the form of a heavier plough and even the three field system.

The manorial system can be sustained only under a relatively egalitarian regime. Otherwise, one must organize elaborate institutions for the exploitation of labor. For example, the decline of population in Italy was inversely correlated to the fortune of war of Rome and to the number of incoming slaves. There is good evidence that Italy was incapable of permanently sustaining a large population under the latifundia system. The manorial

---

* Slicher van Bath, *An Agrarian History of Europe*, translated by Olive Ordish, 1963, pp. 40–59, 69–74.
† Gibbon, *the Decline and Fall of the Roman Empire*.
‡ Bloch, *op. cit.*
§ E. Boserup, *The Conditions of Agricultural Growth*, Aldine (Chicago, 1965).
** Latouche, ch. III of *The Birth of Western Economy*, Barnes and Noble (New York, 1961).

system can be seen as the most that can be done for an upper class in the absence of a slave economy.

Even so, the Germanic style of agriculture put narrow constraints on the extent of the inequality of income distribution. In a pastoral state, the dispersion of population and paucity of surplus make difficult any great central power. Why should the Barbarian of the forest submit himself to another's authority? This was the background of the Germanic tribes when they came in conflict with the Roman legions. Centuries later, they tried to obtain for themselves some of the benefits of civilization. Being numerous, the tribes divided the West into many parts. The process of decentralization is not unlike that in other times and after other empires. Successful bandits became successful conquerors. Dividing the spoils, they obliterate centralized power, the primary aspect of the empire. Finding themselves in the unaccustomed position of slave owners, they watch the slaves gradually die, uncognizant of the fact that they must be ever recruited from neighboring nations. Indeed, the whole notion of slavery is strange and unnatural. The empire is compromised by the failure of road maintenance, regional taxes on traffic, and inadequate protection against thieving knights. But this is of no great impact since the urban population is dwindling and so the need for long term transport.

The Merovingian (466–75) and Carolingian (751–987) dynasties might be thought to represent attempts to restore something of the old order. However, accounts of its economic and political organization make it clear that at their strongest, these were the familiar folk-nations, and at their weakest, they were loose confederations lead by the chief bandit turned conquerer.

The Germanic invasion and the institutional changes thereby wrought forced a redistribution of income to labor and away from the aristocracy. Naturally, the pattern of trade changed. There was a decline in the market for luxuries, goods which are purchased by the aristocracy, whereas the market for the basic staples increased.

Since only the demand for luxuries can maintain industries which benefit from an extensive division of labor, the redistribution of labor will lead to a decline in inter-regional trade. Therefore, the decline in trade after the fall of the Roman empire can be as easily attributed to the redistribution of income as to impediments to trade raised by the Mohammedans* or to the destruction of capital and the ignorance in manufacturing of the Germans.

---

* Pirenne, *Medieval Cities: Their Origins and the Revival of Trade*, Princeton, 1925.

6*

As such, the manorial system appears to be the one favored by the Carolingians. Lopez postulates that this was pat of an overall system of government designed to avoid the fate of the Merovingians who impoverished themselves by surrendering land to their subjects in return for services against their enemies.* Instead, the Carolingians, granted land in return for continuous service. Should the vassal fail to provide the service owed, the land reverted to the owner. Hence, the lord need not give new land to obtain services. From an economic viewpoint, the Carolingians were expressing preference for longer term benefits. Presumably, they would have obtained more services initially by an outright grant. Instead they preferred to accept fewer services at first but more later.

One element of the manorial system suggests an origin more ancient than the Carolingians. The system set obligations and granted rightsg according to birth. Certainly, the idea of blood inheritance was strong among the early Germans. There was in Northwest European no monarch of peasant descent. Of course, there were many disputed thrones but the question of legitimacy through birth was important even in the early tribes. This is in contrast to the Roman or Chinese empires where peasants were elevated to emperor. It was the imperial army from which the peasant emperors were recruited or from which they seized the sceptar. In contrast, European armies were lead by the nobility. This notion of inheritance by blood permeated the whole feudal society, so that normally the lands of serfs and lords alike passed to the first son. Only if the vassal's son defaulted on his obligations would the vassalage be defaulted and passed on to another. In contrast, the Roman or Chinese aristocrat could adopt a son or pass inheritance to a friend or distant relative.

2 AGRICULTURAL TECHNOLOGY AND ECONOMIC ORGANIZATION

There were three main developments in Medieval agriculture. By the 6th century, strip cultivation was developed by means of the wheel plough with fixed mouldboard.† As compared with the square fields of antiquity, the strips were immune to erosion. Hence, they allowed long term agriculture in the wet climate of Northwest Europe. The investment in the plough was a

---

* Lopez, *op. cit.*
† Slicher van Bath, *op. cit.*, p. 64.

small one and hence for all practical purposes, land and labor were the primary factors of production.

By the 8th century, there were adoptions of the three field crop rotation, whereby one field was sown with winter grain, one with spring gain, and one fallow.* Formerly, in the Mediterannean, there was the two field system whereby one field was sown with winter grain and another lay fallow. Evidently, precipitation was inadequate for a successful spring crop.

Output from seed of three to four to one appears to be the rule in the late middle ages.† If one fourth of output were devoted to seed, a change to a three field system would cost one half of output for one year. This would appear to be a very small investment in view of the return. Still labor and land were the primary factors of productions.

The output of winter grain would be $\frac{2}{3}$ of the former level whereas that of spring grain would be more or less $\frac{2}{3}$ of the former quantity of spring grain. Let p_s be the value of spring grain for output from an acre of land and let p_w be the value of winter grain for an acre of output. Roughly speaking

$$\tfrac{2}{3}(p_w + p_s) > p_w$$

$$p_s > \tfrac{1}{2}p_w$$

would be a minimal condition for changing from a two field system to a three field system. Of course, the greater p_s, the greater the incentive to change. Since spring grain included oats and barley, the greater the demand for beer (and malt) and the larger the number of horses, the greater p_s.‡

By the 10th century, the horse collar permitted the use of horses in ploughing. The horse provided much more power than the ox and hence the number of man hours per acre of cultivation was reduced. This opened up the opportunity to exploit heretofore marginal lands. Also, the horse was a heavy consumer of oats which promoted the three field system. This connection between the collar and the three field system has been noted in historical research.§

Undoubtedly, the horse represented a major investment. In England in 1250–1400, horses of ordinary quantity sold for about one third a year's wages of a thatcher and a fourth of a year's wages of a carpenter.** Never-

---

* *Ibid.*
† *Ibid.*
‡ *Ibid.*, p. 64.
§ *Ibid.*, and White, Lynn. *op. cit.*
** I. G. T. Rogers, *A History of Agriculture and Prices in England 1259–1400*, Oxford at the Clarendon Press, 1866, reprinting by Kraus Reprint, Inc., Vaduz, 1963.

theless, before extensive use of horses, the market was limited by the maximum natural rate of reproduction whereas afterwards no further accumulation was necessary. Ignoring outside supplies (the Arabs) or drains (the military), the horse was much like the land: a natural and not easily manipulated asset. Capital as an asset which was readily accumulated did not play a major role in the agricultural economy. An exception would be buildings but even these would be limited by land and animals. Like the three field system, the drainage of swamps or the cutting of forests was a once-and-for-all investment limited by the available land. Perhaps the investment was undertaken by young men just before marriage when the loss of income could be borne. Such investments offered limited opportunities for land speculators, but the largest investment of capital was in the water and windmills and in millstones. These too were limited by the extent of the land. In the period, 1250–1400, in England the average imported millstone cost from a half to three quarters of a years wages of a thatcher and about one third to one half the average yearly wage of a carpenter.* This was about three times the price of an ox.

In summary, agricultural techniques in the middle ages did not give much opportunity for direct capitalization. In turn, institutional arrangements were not conducive to the development of capital intensive technologies. Indeed, later history indicated that the greatest returns to agriculture might have been from capital devoted to research in agricultural techniques. Prior to the 18th century, progress in agriculture was indeed slight. For example yields did not improve between the 14th and 18th centuries. In many areas, agriculture became more intense and there was a decrease in grazing of land and forests, but yields remained static. The next stage of progress was occasioned by the application of modern science to obtain mechanization, chemical fertilizers, and improved animal and plant strains. It is doubtful that any agriculture system would have accomplished such improvements in the middle ages. Certainly the feudal system did not.

In Merovingian and Carolingian times, the serf provided up to half of his labor to the lord.† In addition the serf supplied certain goods in kind. Hence, the amount of time left to the serfs' own disposal was not great. Furthermore, should he perform his obligations to the dissatisfaction of the lord, he would be replaced. Also, any experiments might be unacceptable to the lord for their lack of current output or for their violation of traditional methods of life. Like the peasant, the lords were not immune to excessive scep-

---

* *Ibid.*   † van Bath, *op. cit.*, p. 48.

ticism and even superstition about finding new methods of production. Therefore, only the lord or free peasant would be expected to carry on experiments
in agriculture. Since the lord was primarily occupied with military technology,
this left only the free peasant. The free peasant was especially vulnerable to
raids by knights or the pagan invaders such as Vikings and Hungarians.
Hence, many of them paid homage to nearly lords in the form of inheritance
taxes (succession taxes), poll taxes (chevage), or event rents.* Indeed in
many cases, the peasants lost their freedom altogether. Under the Merovingians, serfs and peasants were but little subject to lords. Though serfs were
legally bound to the land as in the Roman times, they could easily run away.
Thus, there were many free peasant. By the time of St. Louis, most of North
France had been transformed to a rather strict form of serfdom. In Germany,
especially in the North and East, many more peasant retained some form of
freedom. After the Norman invasion, serfdom was perhaps dominant in
South and Central England.

In the late Middle Ages, there was a gradual shift from the manorial
system to tenant farming.† This event opened up the possibility of a greater
capitalization of agriculture. Still it was several centuries before the peasant
was secure in his rights to the product of the land.

Technical progress in agriculture in the late Middle Ages was not unlike
that in the earlier period, except that the later developments were less
spectacular.‡ The Oriental windmill was improved to give a source of power
for flat areas. A lighter wheel plough was developed. In certain areas, the
scythe replaced the sickle—which was labor saving but more expensive of
storage space and hauling. In each case, the saving of labor could be attained
with a modest investment, and once done, there was no further advantage
to capital accumulation.

The movement from payment in kind (including labor) to sharecropping
and/or rents ultimately undermined feudal society. Hence, there has been a
great deal of speculation as to its cause. Dobb has advanced the thesis that
the downfall of Feudalism was due to its inefficiency in raising revenues
for the upper classes.§ Therefore, the lords abolished the manorial system

---

* Bloch, Marc, *Feudal Society*, University of Chicago Press, Chicago, Illinois, 1961,
   pp. 169–175, 255–274.
† van Bath, *op. cit.*, pp. 145–141.
‡ *Ibid*, pp. 183–189.
§ Dobb, *Studies in the Development of Capitalism* (New York, 1947). For further refine-
   ments, see comments by Dobb and Sweezy, In Sweezy ed., *The Transition from Feudalism to Capitalism*, (*Science and Society*), New York, 1954.

and the economic basis of political bondage was undermined. According to a modern version of the Dobb thesis offered by Bowman, population growth reduced the wage rate to the extent that the lords found it more profitable to use hired labor or share cropping instead of depending upon obligations fixed in kind:* products in kind were a declining portion of growing output and labor services were falling in value. Certainly, in England in the late middle ages, there was a large reserve of cheap agricultural labor descended from the younger sons of serfs.†

A contrary view is that of Pirenne who has argued that feudalism developed when the trade routes to the East were cut off and declined as the European cities grew as a replacement for the East.‡ According to this theory, the cities forced a free labor market and caused a breakage of the bondage aspect of feudalism. Since it is not at all clear that the burghers would have the power to abolish the system, one might find the Dobb explanation of some interest. In particular, the notion that the lords were willing collaborators in the abolition of the systems is attractive, and considering the structure of government say in England is not too far from the facts. On the other hand, a motive must be found and the instruments of power must be specified.

In particular, it is not sufficient merely to prove that the lords were dissatisfied with the system. It must be shown that it was in their interest to release labor from the manors.

Factors in the late middle ages favorable to modifications of feudal obligations were:

1) The use of the horse for ploughing reduced the demand for labor by the lords. Hence, labor services rendered were not as highly valued.
2) Falling real wage rates for agricultural labor not bound to the land.
3) The reduction in the necessity of home defense which would allow the lords to fight abroad. Especially, the Crusades would have encouraged more reliance on the initiative of the peasants.

However, according to Rogers, a 19th century English economist and statistician, in the century before the black death, 1250–1350, real rural

---

* John Bowman, "On Dobb and the Breaking of European Feudalism, "mimeo. 1966.
† Clapham, *A Concise History of Britain*, Cambridge University Press, 1957.
‡ Pirenne, *Medieval Cities: Their Origins and the Revival of Trade*, Princeton, 1925.

wages were falling but afterwards, they were rising.* This can be seen in Table 1 where real wage calculations are made from Rogers' data. Before 1340, there appears to be an inconstant downward trend in real wages but afterwards an increase. An exception occurs during the last part of the century at the time of the English peasants revolt in 1381, when England had suffered grieviously from the exigencies of the Hundred Years War. These trends are common to all the indices except the wage/wool index. Possibly wool prices were exceptionally slow in increasing since much of the wool was exported to Flanders. During the plague, the demand for wool by Flander undoubtedly fell. As an intermediate product, the fall in demand for wool may have more than offset the fall in its supply. Yet the greatest change in conditions in tenure were after the Black death. Indeed, they were accompanied by the peasant revolts, both before and after the Black death.†
In the low countries, on the North Sea and in Switzerland, many areas were transformed so that peasants had a measure of self rule. Their grievances included the arbitrariness of the lords' justice and the low return to labor Hence, it is doubtful that the transfer from obligations in kind was invariably motivated by the lords' interests. Indeed new factors had entered, in particular, the peasant wars in the areas where the bourgeosie was powerful. It will be seen that this was no coincidence. For example in 1301, the Londoners joined John Ball's peasants in revolt against the lords.

To turn to perhaps the most difficult issue in medieval agriculture history, what were the rules of distribution of the products of the land? Evidently, the legal rules constantly changed. Were there underlying economic principles of distribution? In one view, feudalism allocated a fixed share to the peasants.‡ However, one must not draw too strictly the analogy between Northwest Europe and say India at the time of the British and French colonization. The Indian village was characterized by distribution by custom from a common output.§ However, with Northwest European feudalism the rules were more complicated and subject to more radical changes.

---

* Rogers, *op. cit.*, similar results are presented in the research of Holmes, *The Estates of the Higher Nobility in Fourteenth Century England*, Cambridge, 1957, Clapham, *op. cit.*, Raftis, *The Estates of Ramsey Abbey*, *Pontifical Institute of Medieval Studies*, Toronto, 1957, In Bath, *op. cit.*, calculations are made from the Winchester estate, Sharply rising wages in the first half of the 14th century found there contradict the constant or falling money wages in other sources.

† van Bath, *op. cit.*, pp. 189–194.

‡ Nicolas, Georgescu-Roegen, "Economic Theory and Agrarian Economics," *Oxford Economic Papers*, XII (1960), 1–40.

§ Walter Neale, *op. cit.*

Table 1   Indices of wage price: 1261–1400

(Source: J. E. T. Rogers, *A History of Agricultural Prices in England*, Vol. I., 1259–1400, Oxford at the Clarendon Press)

	Wheat threshing[1] /Wheat	Reaping /Wheat	Wheat threshing[1] /Boars	Wheat threshing[1] /Wool	Wheat threshing[1] /Eggs
1261–1270	100	100	100	100	100
1271–1280	81	76	56	94	87
1281–1290	100	87	38	107	98
1291–1300	83	74	51	120	95
1301–1310	91	79	32	105	82
1311–1320	84	68	54	111	90
1321–1330	79	75	66	107	82
1331–1340	108	116	66	130	76
1341–1350	109	102	89	154	94
1351–1360	90	94	119	156	79
1361–1370	98	89	82	105	122
1371–1380	136	158	102	143	116
1381–1390	115	174	76	138	100
1391–1400		117	55	135	100

[1]   East England

Since there were a large number of lords and peasants and since rights of peasants to the land were not guaranteed, one would expect the lords to be able to apply considerable pressure. If wages fell, the lords designed new schemes for obtaining a larger share of output. For example, they began to apply wage labor to the demesne and in return for services of serfs not needed, they obtained money rents. After the black death, the peasants revolted in an effort to obtain the more favorable terms justified by the the shortage of labor.

As has been mentioned with regard to the Dobb thesis, the share of the lords did not remain constant as output increased. Since a change was forthcoming and since economic reality favored the attainment of a competitive wage rather than a share fixed by tradition but violated by the letter of the laws, there was a tendency to a competitive wage for serfs. Nevertheless, the mechanism was crude and slow moving so that one must not think that there was always a equalization of wages between free labor and the serfs. Rather distribution of the lands' produce would fall between certain bounds set by competitive conditions.

The comparision between the constant share and competitive theory can be seen most clearly in the case of a single product, given by a production function:

$$q = f(L, N_1),$$

where L is land and N_1 is agricultural labor. Denote the marginal products by

$$f_{N_1} = \frac{\partial q}{\partial N_1}$$

$$f_L = \frac{\partial q}{\partial L}$$

and the rate of change of the marginal products by

$$f_{N_1 N_1} = \frac{\partial^2 q_2}{\partial N_1}$$

$$f_{N_1 L} = \frac{\partial^2 q}{\partial N_1 \partial L_1} = \frac{\partial^2 q}{\partial L \partial N_1} = f_{LN_1} \text{ (Young's theorem)}$$

$$f_{LL} = \frac{\partial^2 q}{\partial L^2}$$

The marginal rate of substitution is the slope of the isoproduct curve in factor space which can be shown to be equal to

$$mrs = \frac{dN_1}{dL}\bigg|_{q \text{ constant}} = -\frac{f_L}{f_{N_1}} \tag{1}$$

(Let $f(N_1, L) = $ constant. Then

$$f_{N_1} \frac{dN_1}{dL} + f_L = 0).$$

In determining the interests of the lords, a key role is played by the *elasticity of substitution*, η_1 which is the recipricol of the relative change in the marginal rate of substitution when a change takes place in the ratio of land to labor.

1 REMARK

$$\eta_1 = \frac{f_L f_{N_1}}{f_{LN_1} f} = \left(\frac{\partial mrs}{\partial (N_1/L)} \frac{N_1/L}{mrs} \right)^{-1}$$

In the case where the marginal rate of substitution equals the relative wage rates, and letting r = rent = f_L on land and w = wage rate = f_{N_1},

$$\frac{N_1/L}{rL/wN_1} = \frac{\partial r/wN_1}{\partial N_1/L} \eta_1^{-1} - 1.$$

Proof

$$\frac{\partial f_L/f_{N_1}}{\partial N_1/L} = L\frac{f_{N_1L}}{f_{N_1}} - \frac{f_{N_1N_1}Lf_L}{f_{N_1}^2}$$

$$= L\frac{f_{N_1L}}{f_{N_1}} + f_{N_1L}\frac{f_LL^2}{f_{N_1}^2N_1}$$

$\Bigg($ by differentiating Eulers' theorem: $f_{N_1} = f_{N_1} + f_{N_1N_1}N_1 + f_{N_1L}L$

or $\qquad f_{N_1N_1} = -f_{N_1L}\left(\dfrac{L}{N_1}\right)\Bigg)$

$$= f_{N_1L}\left(\frac{L}{f_{N_1}} + \frac{f_LL}{f_{N_1}f_{N_1}N_1}L\right)$$

$$= f_{N_1L}\left(\frac{L}{f_{N_1}} + \frac{L}{f_{N_1}}\left(\frac{f - f_{N_1}N_1}{f_{N_1}N_1}\right)\right)$$

(Eulers' theorem)

$$= \frac{f_{N_1L}f}{f_Lf_{N_1}}\frac{Lf_L}{f_{N_1}N_1}.$$

$$\frac{\partial f_LL/f_{N_1}N_1}{\partial N_1/L} = \frac{\partial f_L/f_{N_1}}{\partial N_1/L}\frac{L}{N_1} - \frac{f_L}{f_{N_1}}\frac{L^2}{N_1^2}$$

$$= \frac{L}{N_1}\left(\frac{\partial f_L/f_{N_1}}{\partial N_1/L} - \frac{f_LL}{f_{N_1}N_1}\right)$$

$$= \frac{L}{N_1}\frac{f_LL}{f_{N_1}N_1}\left(\frac{f_{N_1L}f}{f_Lf_{N_1}} - 1\right).$$

q.e.d.

As labor increases, the land share of output will increase if $\eta_1 < 1$, decrease if $\eta_1 > 1$ and remain the same if $\eta_1 = 1$. Hence if $\eta_1 = 1$, the competitive wage and fixed serf share theories are qualitatively the same. In recent times, η_1 is about one.* In Feudal times, there was less opportunity

* Griliches, "Agricultural Production Functions," *American Economic Review*, **54** (1964), 961–974.

for substitution of land for labor so that $\eta_1 < 1$. According to the competitive wage theory, the serf share of a given field should have decreased as population on the land increased. Certainly the wage rate fell (Table 1) and the commutation of feudal obligations to money rents would indicate an effort to obtain a larger share for land. Competitive wages for serfs together with $\eta_1 < 1$ would provide an explanation for a change from serfdom to tenancy. (With $\eta_1 \geq 1$, more serfs could be brought onto the land at the old or reduced obligations and still equilibrium would have been maintained with the labor market).

If a rising labor-land ratio led to a change in the crop mix, then one must restrict attention to shares of money income. Nevertheless, the extent to which crop shifts could be made to increase labor intensity was limited, since wealth was low enough to make grains of a similar and standardized nature the basic staple of life.

3 URBAN ECONOMIC ORGANIZATION AND TECHNOLOGY

In the Middle Ages, a degree of division of labor had led to the gathering of free artisans in villages among the manors and farms—blacksmiths, carpenters, masons, slaters, sawyers, tilers, and others. Their activities were more or less proportional to the extent of agricultural output. Hence, they are to be regarded as part of the agricultural system. Also, there were many fishing villages which provided a product more or less like that of agriculture proper—usable to provide the necessities of life and harvested by labor from nature. Probably capital was important but as in agriculture proper, there were severe limitations on the amount of capital which could be profitably utilized.

In contrast, in larger towns commerce and manufacturing were oriented to markets outside the town's immediate boundaries. Here there were many new technical developments requiring large capital outlays. What is more, the possibility of long run trade gave a still greater opportunity for accumulated capital.

In both exported and manufactured goods, the town offered mainly luxuries, the intermediate products for luxuries, and the day to day needs of its own inhabitants. An exception might be metals which were refined and used in agricultural implements. In effect, towns were villagers plus trade plus small luxury manufacturing establishments in contrast to the agricultural community which equalled village plus farm.

From a register of 1363 in Nuremberg, of 1200 masters, 9% were employed in luxury trades (furrier, mantle makers, and coach builders), 7% in more or less military services (mail glove makers, briddle, spur, and stirrup makers, saddlers, blade makers, sword-polishers, helmet-smiths and mail-shirt makers), 4% in construction (carpenters; cabinet-makers; rope makers; stone-masons; and nail makers), 12% in metal (braziers, belt makers, tin founders, tinkers, farriers, tool-makers, tin, smiths, pewters, ironers, sheet metal workers, polishers).* 30% were in clothing and related products. The rest were in various services and "necessities" of life oriented mainly to the needs of the citizenry.

Large scale cloth industries existed in Flanders and Florence at least.† Textiles were a major industry in the low countries, Italy, and perhaps South Germany. The products produced, silk, cotton, linen and fine woolens, were marketed to the upper class. The technology of textiles was such as to offer great opportunity for capital accumulation and hence in the late Middle Ages the organization of the textile industry was prophetic of that which was to come. The draw loom borrowed from the near East formed the basis of small silk industry and the more extensive linen, cotton and woolen industries.‡ Also, the fulling mill, driven by a water mill, gradually replaced the treading of cloth in vats. This development was highly labor saving. In the late Middle Ages, the spindle and the flyer supplemented the loom. These inventions were perhaps modest in their requirements of capital, even if one adds to the list organizational economies which may have accompanied relatively large scale operations. (The latter might require some working capital for steady and consistent payment of wages). Nevertheless, there was extensive opportunity for capital simply because the textile industries were slowly developing in Northwest Europe.

What is more, many more inventions of a capital intensive nature occured in the 15th and 16th centuries, especially in terms of applying mechnical power to the spindle and the flyer and knitting. Leonardo de Vinci's contributions were of particular note. Hence, the textile industry presented opportunity for capital for many years to come.

To an even greater extent than in textiles, the water wheel improved mining operations by giving a means for transporting ore and water for the mine. In turn the mines provided the metal for mechanical developments.

---

* Klem, *op. cit.*, pp. 95–98.
† *Ibid.*, p. 86.
‡ Abbot Payson Usher, *A History of Mechanical Inventions*, revised edition, Harvard U. Press, Harvard, Mass., 1954, Ch. XI.

For example, firearms, lathes, clocks and the gears of water wheels and windmills sooner or later utilized metal, especially iron and steel.* Mining was most important in Italy, Germany, and Flanders, although it must have been extensive over most of Northwest Europe.† Just as in the case of textiles, mining was more fully developed in the Renaissance. Hence, there was ample opportunity for capital accumulation.

The change in major military technology in the early Middle ages related to horse riding; spurs from Arabs countries, horseshoes in the ninth century, and the stirrup and bridle from central Asia.‡ These contributed to the development of cavalry and to the dominance of the military class, thereby strengthening the lords in their holdings. Indeed, the cavalry was the focus of chivalry and was the dominant force in putting down peasant revolts in the 14th and 15th centuries. From a more pedestrian view point, there was a major industry devoted to servicing the military. In the late middle ages, gun powder from China was utilized to develop artillery and small firearms.§ Obviously, in subsequent centuries, there were ever more complex developments.

Architecture and stone masonry reached levels of acheivement never equalled, before or since.** The construction of tapestries and other cloth work reached similar heights. These were mainly for the use of the military elite and church. In business, the keeping of accounts reached a high degree of development, especially with double entry bookkeeping in 12th century Italy.†† The keeping of such records is essential if one is to judge the efficiency of capital accumulation. In transportation in the 12th century, there was developed a sailing ship needing no oarsmen.‡‡ Also, there appeared an improved rudder and in the 13th century the compass was introduced from the Far East. More extensive timber planking to allow larger ships and the carved style sailing-ship became important after the 14th century. These improved the opportunities for capital partially by providing labor saving devices and partially by making investments less sensitive to risk and natural disaster. Again, the expansion afterwards indicates the full opportunity for utilizing capital.

---

* *Ibid.*, ch. XIV, and Klemm, *op. cit.*, Parts two and three.

† Klemm, *op. cit.*, Part Three.

‡ White, *op. cit.*

§ Klemm, *op. cit.*, Part Two.

** Lopez, *op. cit.*

†† Sombart, *Der moderne Kapitalismus* (2nd. ed., München, Duncker und Hunbolt, 1916).

‡‡ Klem, *op. cit.*, pp. 84–85.

Later, in the Renaissance, a new industry appeared, namely printing.
Two conslusions can be drawn:

1) The towns offered ample opportunity for investment. This was borne
out in later years.

2) The towns obtained their food supplies mainly by serving the lords.*

The economic organization of towns in Flanders centered around the
guilds.† At first regulation by the municiple authority was aimed at protecting the public from strikes, fraud, and negligence. The artisans were organized in guilds and they soon limited entry into the profession, forebade
invention, fixed prices, regulated work time, and forebade hiring large
numbers of workmen. On the other hand, the great industries such as
textiles were left to their own, since their owners were rather prominent in
local government. In the 12th and 13th century, they had dominant position.
After the governments passed over to the guilds in the 13th and 14th centuries, the towns began to pursue protectionist policies against the outside.
New competing towns tended to undermine their attempts at monopoly.
The economic center finally shifted from Flanders north, first to Antwerp
and then to Holland.

In England, the guilds never gained so much power as to be a serious
threat to commerce.‡ Adding to the two preceding conclusions,

3) most migrants to a town were excluded from the guilds and hence
tended to be thrown into more menial jobs or into industry. There
was a delay in the full effect of migration on urban output.

4) Otherwise, the division of urban income was along more or less
competitive lines.

5) There was greater opportunity for capital accumulation in new
industries or for established capitalists.

To the extent that the capitalists produced for competitive markets, the
capitalist share of output would tend to zero only in at the extremes of zero
or infinite labor supplies.

The output of the urban areas is assumed to be given by various firms
which operate according to production functions.

$$g(K, N_2)$$

---

* A contrary view is expressed in Bucher, *Etudes d'historie et d'economie politique*,
Paris-Bruxelles, 1901.

† Pirenne, *Early Democracies in the Low Countries*, Harper & Row, 1963.

‡ Clapham, *op. cit.*, p. 132, and Sylvia Thrupp, "Medieval Guilds Reconsidered,"
Journal of Economic History, 164–173, 1942.

where K is the vector of capital stocks and N_2 is the labor in enterprise. The marginal products are denoted

$$\frac{\partial^2 g}{\partial K} = g_K$$

$$\frac{\partial g}{\partial N_2} = g_{N_2}$$

and the rate of change of the marginal products by

$$\frac{\partial^2 g}{\partial K^2} = g_{KK}$$

$$\frac{\partial^2 g}{\partial N_2^2} = g_{N_2 N_2}$$

$$\frac{\partial^2 g}{\partial K_2 N_2} = g_{K_2 N_2}$$

Let $\beta_i g$

be the total of agricultural goods used as raw materials in the ith urban enterprises; β_i is normally a vector. Let p^1 be the vector of prices of agricultural goods, p^2 of urban goods. Let the enterprise produce the ith good, then $p_i^2 g_i - p^1 \beta_i g_i$ is *value added* and $(p_i^2 - p_i^1 \beta_i)$ is *value added per unit output.*

Assume that the producer acts as a classical competitive profit maximizer. The capitalists maximize their incomes which sum to total output minus outlays to raw materials minus the wage bill,

$$p^2 g_i - p^1 \beta g_i - w N_2^i,$$

where w is now the urban wage rate. The first order maximizing condition is

$$(p^2 - p^1 \beta_i) g_{N_2 i} = w \tag{3}$$

Profits are given by the residual:

$$(p^2 g_i - p^1 \beta_i g_i - N_2^i (p^2 - p^1 \beta_i) g_{N_2 i}$$
$$= (p_i^2 - p^1 \beta_i) g_i - N_2^i (p_i^2 - p^1 \beta_i) g_{N_2 i} \tag{3a}$$

For example, if there are constant returns to scale, g is homogeneous of degree 1 and Eulers' theorem applies:

$$g_i = g_K K^i + g_{N_2} N_2^i, \tag{4}$$

so that profits are given by

$$(p_i^2 - p^1\beta_i)g_K K^i$$

The ratio of profits to wages is

$$\frac{g_K K^i}{g_{N_2} N_2^i}.$$

In the case of monopoly, marginal revenue $\equiv mr_i = \dfrac{d(p^2 - p^1\beta_i)g_i}{dg_i}(p - p_1\beta_i).$

Hence, the producer sets

$$mr_i \, g_{N_2 i} = w. \tag{3b}$$

In this most general case,

$$\delta = \frac{d \text{ value added per unit output}}{dg} < 0$$

and

$$mr_i = (p_i^2 - p^1\beta_i) + (p_i^2 - p^1\beta_i)\,\delta$$

$$< p_i^2 - p^1\beta_i.$$

2   REMARK

For the enterprise, so long as K^i and N_2^i are finite, g_K and g_{N_2} are not zero, so that the ratio of profits to wages is neither zero nor infinity. This is a property which will be used.

The state of affairs for investment is similar between competition and monopoly. For a given capital investment, so long as the excess of output over that without the investment, when summed over time, exceeds the cost of the investment, there is a positive rent low enough to justify the investment. From remarks 2 and 1,

3   REMARK

If the townsmen were willing to invest at low but positive rates of return, capital would accumulate indefinitely.

4   REMARK

With indefinite opportunity for investment, the average product of urban output tends to infinity as urban labor tends to to zero and to zero as urban labor tends to infinity.

4 FEUDAL DEMOGRAPHY

As far back into European history as is known, net population changes in towns or cities have been negative or zero whereas they have been positive in the countryside. Two cases in point are early 19th century Sweden* and late 15th century Barcelona.† In the latter case, urban deaths not attributable to plague outweighed urban deaths. Even if the plague were a temporary disaster, there was negative urban population growth.

The particular determinants of birth and death rates are of interest. Birth rates would depend upon the age composition of the population, the per capita consumption of food, and social customs. For example, in England, a young man would not marry until he had a means of support for a family.‡ On the other hand, death rates are corrolated to per capita calorie intake and the density of population. For a relatively well-to-do family in the towns, deaths might outweigh births in urban areas and for a very poor family in the country, death rates might outweigh birth rates.

If payments to labor fall below a certain limit, there is a higher death rate due to malnutrition. For convenience sake, define the *real wage* to be the quantity of agricultural goods (or calories) which can be purchased with a particular wage rate. (The *nominal wage* is defined to be the quantity of urban goods which can be purchased with a particular wage rate). There are three relevant boundaries for real wages. First, if wages in the rural sectors are equal to or above the *malnutrition level*, α, there are no (rural) deaths beyond those due to natural causes and contagious diseases. As the wage rate falls below the malnutrition level, the death rate rises until one reached the *subsistence level*, where net rural population increase is zero. The definition is applied to the rural sector alone, since urban population increase is always negative. Finally, wages can fall further toward infinity until the *zero level*, where labor receives no reward whatever. Of course, the zero wage is only a limiting case.

Recalling section 11 of chapter 1, the paradox of unbalanced growth applies: the ratio of urban population to rural population decreased over time. First, reproduction rates would increase indefinitely as wages tended

---

*   Heckscher, "Swedish Population Trends Before the Industrial Revolution," *Economic History Review*, 2nd series, 2, (1950), pp. 266–277.
†   Robert, S. Smith, "Barcelona'bills of mortality' and population, 1457–1590," *Journal of Political Economy*, 44, 84–93, 1936.
‡   J. C. Russell, "The Plague Population of England," *The Journal of British Studies*, V (1966), 1–21.

to zero. Second, reproduction rates were bounded by the biological maximum. Third, all capital in urban sectors could be accumulated indefinitely from urban output which could increase urban output to a very high level—provided one could meet the urban raw material demands. Fourth, urban outputs were limited by raw materials from the rural areas. Fifth, rural output could tend to infinity, whereupon average product would tend to zero. Sixth, so long as urban wages were bounded from zero, so were profits (remark 2). If accumulation of capital is bounded from zero, so long as there are positive profits, urban capital stocks will grow indefinitely. Note that this is a Protestant ethic type behavior in the sense that the fall in the maximal return of capital does not cut off altogether accumulation from profits.

5 REMARK

So long as capitalists will invest at a positive return, capital stock will grow indefinitely whenever wages are bounded from zero.

Proof It is necessary to show only that at positive wages, the return to capital is positive. From the last section, the marginal return to capital is mrg_K. So long as K is finite, g_K is positive. By equation (3b) and the fact that wages are positive, $mr > 0$. Hence, the marginal return to capital is positive.

q.e.d.

Data on population is extremely hard to obtain. Only in England is population data in the 11th to 14th centuries derived from relatively universal poll taxes. Clapham[*] states that total English population increased by about two thirds from 1100 to 1350. Russell makes a more substantial claim of a three fold increase.[†] On the other hand, the urban labor force is even harder to estimate since much of the labor force of the small towns was devoted to agricultural pursuits.[‡] Therefore, it seems best to take the population of London alone. Russell's data shows that London and the larger towns preserved their same population, one to the other, over the period.[§] Russell estimates this to have increased by four. Williams feels that the increase is too great—on intuitive ground.[**]

---

[*] Clapham, *op. cit.*, pp. 77–78.
[†] J. C. Russell, *British Medieval Population* (Albuquerque, 1948).
[‡] Lipson, *The Economic History of England*, *Vol. I*, *The Middle Ages*, 12th Edition, Barnes and Noble, New York, (1959).
[§] Russell, *op. cit.*, 50–55.
[**] Gwyn A. Williams, *Medieval London*, Anthlone Press, University of London, 1903, pp. 315–317.

Using Russell's 1100 figures for London, one would interpret Thrupp* as claiming that the increase was merely by a factor of two and again Williams claims that Thrupp's estimates are too low, but should be not less than 10,000. This is all confused by the fact that Peter de Blois in 1199 told Pope Innocent III that London had 40,000 people.† If one believed Blois, very little population growth took place in London in the century and a half, 1200–1350. On the other hand, rural population growth was quite rapid in this period.‡ Of course, this is the relevant period of analysis, after the system had had time to move to the long run equilibrium and was subject only to the force of capital accumulation. It is at least possible that the ratio for urban to rural population fell, whether or not total urban population grew.

5 POLITICAL POWER

The power of feudalism lay with the church, through ideas and religion, and with the lords, through the exercize of military and administrative prerogatives. Outside of the city of Rome, the church appears to have played the role of advisor and preacher rather than that of priest-king. The technology of war favored the horseman and the general level of poverty assured that the horsemen would be few in number. The stirrup led to a new form of war in which the cavalry was the most important single unit of the army.§ Indeed only after Charlamagne, as cavalry became more important, did feudalism take on its distinctive character. Once artillery and infantry took predominance, the chances improved for the bourgeosie and peasantry against the lords.

A particular lord exercized his rights in several ways First he judged his subordinates—with some constraints ** Second, he owned directly consider-

---

* Thrupp, *The Merchant Class of Medieval London.*
† Williams, *op. cit.*, p. 317.
‡ See Clapham. *op. cit.*, p. 77. This view is reinforced by studies of Litow, "Some Evidence of the Thirtheenth Century Population Increase." *Economic History Review*, 14, (1961–1962), pp. 218–224.
§ White, *Medieval Technology and Social Charge*, Oxford, 1962 argues that cavalry was relatively unimportant until the time of Charles Mantel and that he risked the confiscation of church lands only because of the great power of the Frankish knights. This is contrary to the thesis that the church tolerated the confiscation to aid the cause against the Saracens, whom White regards as having been weak relative to the Franks. Hence, Brunner's theory of the origin of Feudalism by Carolingian intent is upheld.
** Bloch, *op. cit.*, Ch. XXVIII.

able land and obligations of labor service. Nevertheless, he was always constrained by the fact that his serfs might run away to the towns or to the frontier. His relative weakness in this regard depended upon social policy: to what extent and in what circumstances could he expect the return of his vassals? Was it necessary to use his remaining personal resources to retrieve them or could he enlist the aid of his fellows? For example, Bloch points out that vassalage was a contract which was not respected whenever either party failed to perform the required service.* Even more serious, were younger sons of serfs to be held on the land or were they to be allowed to leave?

To the extent that there were advantage to the individual lords of collective decisions, to that extent there were instruments of class power.

Individual lords would seek to maximize the number of serfs under their control. For the class it might be otherwise. Indeed, social policies might affect lords differentiably according to their wealth or location. A particular lord might even find that his most natural interest lay with the bourgeosie or even the peasantry. Nevertheless, most lords were distinguished from the rest of the population by their military and administrative skill and lack of talents in commerce, agriculture, and farming.

As a class, the military strength of the lords and their knights gave them doninance. Theirs was the power to pillage the towns, to return serfs to the lord, and ultimately to decide the status of the peasantry. Only in a few areas could the towns offer strong resistance. Elsewhere, only the organization of lords as a class constrained them from exercizing their great powers. This fact is underlined by the experience of France in the Hundred Years War when central authority held little power. French knights pillaged the French countryside without successful opposition from their victims.† Only class interest as exercized by the overlords or Parliaments could regulate the aristocrats.

Obviously, for any particular lord, it is always to his advantage to keep as much labor as possible on his lands, so long as the marginal contribution of the labor exceeds its marginal cost of being sustained. Yet throughout the feudal period, the peasants were able to enjoy a certain level of income

---

* Bloch, *op. cit.*, Ch. XXXII.
† *The Hundred Years War*, from the selection work of Jean Le Bel, Jean Froissant & Enguerrand de Montrelet, translated by P. E. Thompson, Folio Society, London, 1966. Also in Froissants' original account, there is recounted the oppression of the 358 Peasant Revolt by the alliances of nobility of France. The knights played the dominant role, charging into mobs of unarmed or poorly armed peasants.

above the subsistence level. This happened in the midst of a great increase in the number of peasants and much movement of population—to the East and to the cities. Therefore, the final outcome was not what it would have been had each lord served his own interest. There are several ways in which the lord was constrained.* First, the younger sons of serfs were born with obligations to the lords but without a share in land equal to that of the eldest, due to the practice of primogeniture.† There was a tendency for serfs to run away to the town and, understandably, the town fathers were not enthusiastic about returning them to their masters. The only way the serfs could be returned was by the rural areas bearing a cost of threatened hostility. Whenever, one lord could not wage the war alone, the interest of the class would be an important determinant of the amount of resources devoted to bringing the serfs back. More important, the laws and obligations on the serfs would be adjusted by pressure from a higher authority, such as an overlord or the ritular king. Presumably, the higher authority would be looking at the intetests of the whole class of lords. For example, in many areas the rule was respected whereby freedom was awarded after residing in the town for a year and a day. Such rules were valid only by the authority of the overlord, as was to prove the case when the towns were reduced in Eastern Europe.

Therefore, there were at least two instruments of control over the flow of population from the countryside to the cities which were wielded by the lords as a class rather that individually. Later, there developed more powerful instruments of social policy, such as Parliament in England and the monarchy in France. Herein lies the explanation of why the marginal value to the lords of the peasantry was not driven to zero as would be required by the interest of any given lord.

Let $\lambda p^1 Q^1$ be the total product accruing to labor, $v p^1 Q^1$ to land, where

$$v + \lambda = 1. \tag{5}$$

Let the total non-agricultural goods entering the market be given by Q^2. If laborers use a percentage of their income, t, for these goods and if it is assumed that land owners spend all their land income on non-agricultural

---

* See E. Lipson, *The Economic History of England, Vol. I., The Middle Ages*, 12th Edition, Barnes and Noble, New York (1959), pp. 92–93, 109–110. Lipson also mentions the development of a free agricultural labor market made up of the younger children of the serfs, a labor market from which the cities would eventually draw. However, this may well represent not the tool of the lords, but an impediment to their power, which eventually aided in the breakup of feudalism.

† Heath, *Economic History of Europe*, Harpers, 1948, pp. 96–97.

goods, then $(\lambda + tv)p^1Q^1$ is delivered to the cities in return for urban goods.* This is called the *agricultural surplus*. The share of urban goods going to the land owners would be the product of their share of the agricultural surplus and total urban output going to agriculture,

$$u = p^2Q^2 \left(\frac{p^1Q^1}{\lambda p^1Q^1 + tvp^1Q^1} \right)$$

$$= p^2Q^2 \frac{\lambda}{\lambda + tv}$$

$$= p^2Q^2 \frac{\lambda}{t + (1 - t)\lambda}. \tag{6}$$

We assume that the interest of the class of lords requires the maximization of this quantity. For example, if t equals zero, the lords try to maximize the flow of urban goods into agriculture.

Some words are in order about the particular maximum here adopted. The interests of the upper classes are often alluded to in accounts of political decisions, especially late in the feudal era. Nevertheless, it is never clear just what the upper class is maximizing. Sometimes, writers quote falling rents as a disaster to the lords. However, according to the position taken here, this would be so only if there was also a decline in urban goods flowing to the lords. In short, not only the quantity of rents but also what they bring on the urban market relates to the interest of the lords. Remembrance of this proposition will help in unravelling some rather complex considerations relating to the interest of the lords.

There remains the question of the horizon of the lords. In the short run, they take total population as given and try to distribute it between the cities and the farms to their advantage. If they take a longer view, they must consider only those urban-rural population combinations which lead to no change in total population. In both the short and the long view, relative urban and agricultural prices are important. In the long view, there is the added population constraint.

Now observe that the agricultural surplus

$$(\lambda + tv)p^1Q^1$$

* For a specification of these goods and the markets for which they were intended, see Pirenne, *Economic and Social History of Medieval Europe*, translated by I. E. Clegg, Harcourt, Grace, & Co. (New York), 1937, pp. 39–43, 140–157, 176–177.

goes to the cities, and therefore in exchange the cities provide a supply of non-agricultural goods of value Q^2. Therefore, the value of urban goods flowing to the cities is equal to the value of the agricultural surplus

$$p^2Q^2 = p^1(\lambda + tv)f.$$

6 REMARK

Lords wish to maximize

$$u = \lambda p^1 Q^1,$$

which is the value of income to land. In the next chapter, it will be necessary to compute the going price of agricultural goods in terms of urban goods.

7 REMARK

Assume that price is given, due perhaps to the fact that most of the goods are marketed in international trade.

Then the lords will seek to increase the labor of the manor until such time as the standard of living is barely adequate for sustaining agricultural population. City population will be allowed to decline indefinitely.

Proof Land income increases as labor increases, since for a given field, land has income

$$p^1 f - p^1 f_{N_1} N_1$$

and

$$\frac{\partial}{\partial N_1} (p^1 f - p^1 f_{N_1} N_1) = p^1 f_{N_1} - p^1 f_{N_1} - p^1 f_{N_1 N_1} N_1$$

$$= -p^1 f_{N_1 N_1} N_1 > 0.*$$

As labor increases, further increases in land income may be possible with shifts in the output mix.

Hence, the lords as a class would wish to have as much labor in agriculture as possible, subject to the constraint of a stable population. They would find no reason at all for allowing an urban population since the urban population normally has a negative rate of growth and therefore must be sustained by an inflow from the countryside. The very inflow presumed a standard of living in the countryside above that which could prevail if labor is increased in quantity. Further increases in population will be stable so that the subsistence agricultural wage will represent the optimum either as the limit of placing all labor on the land or as the object of conscious, long run policy.

q.e.d.

---

* Here p^1 can be taken to be value added after subtracting raw material costs as explained on page 100.

Remark 7 gives an explanation of the resurgence of feudalism in East Europe, where by geographical accident, the lords remained dominant, and later the development of a Europe-wide market destroyed their incentive for collaboration with the cities. Also it illustrated what might have happened had the impediments to Eastern trade not encouraged the growth of the cities.*

The thesis is well illustrated in the Prussian case where, in the 14th century, at the time when West Europe feudalism was beginning to weaken, the Prussian towns declined and the peasants were reduced to serfdom.† In the Prussian case, by various means, the lords acquired the heriditary, pre-feudal judgeships. Thereafter the peasants were at their mercy. The cities also came under the dominance of the lords and they were allowed to decline. Without any class reason for the cities, feudalism was fully established and was not abolished until 1807, about the time of the first opportunity for further capital investments in agriculture.

6 FEUDALISM AS AN ECONOMIC SYSTEM

It remains to show that the descriptions offered above are mutually compatable. Then there is the question as to its efficiency. Finally, did Feudalism adhere to the standards of distributive justice?

In its economic aspects, the agricultural sector was competitive with some supplementary traditional obligations. All these are within the usual view of pure competition. The obligations can be incorporated into the initial wealth distribution and payments in kind can be regarded as worth their market value. Likewise, the urban economy was basically competitive with possibly some monopolistic elements. Monopolists generally take other prices as given and then set their output to maximize profits. Demographically, labor reproduction depended upon real wages. Politically, the flow of labor from the countryside to the city was regulated to maximize the flow of goods to the lords. Hence, there were prices, quantities of goods, labor reproduction, and labor migration from which are derived, excess demands, quantities of goods, labor production, and labor migration. There is a socioeconomic system. The excess demands and other outcomes are ordinarily upper semi-continuous correspondences as maximizers of continuous

---

* This point is due to Werner Hochwald.

† Herbert Tuttle, *History of Prussia to the accession of Frederic the Great, 1134–1740*, Hougton, Miffin & Co., Boston, Mass, 1884, Ch. II.

(utility) functions on the continuous correspondences of alternatives—given prices and other variables. Indeed, only the budget set for the consumers is a great difficulty. For it to be continuous, it is sufficient that there be a set of goods which all like in ever larger quantities and that even persons driven to the level of imminent death be able to sacrifice at least one of these goods.* All the other sets from which "agents" choose, e.g. production possibility sets, or rates of reproduction are straightforward continuous correspondences of the underlying social conditions. Walras' law holds and a good which all prefer in larger quantities, e.g. golden goblets, will assure condition 4) of theorem 13, Section 8 of chapter 1.

8 REMARK

Socio-economic equilibrium exists for feudalism-as described. By modifying economic relationships, Feudalism slows the adjustment to changes in economic conditions. However, the slowing tends to divide the countryside and the towns into separate entities. Within the confines of either of these communities, adjustment would be quick and because of the simplicity of their economies, straightforward.

Assuming equal production functions on each manor and equal proportional population growth between manors, the labor distribution would effectively remain in equilibrium as the lords absorbed the serfs in equal proportion, and the market for goods would be the only one left to equilibrate its price. Presumably, goods prices would move directly to the equilibrium level. Complicated multiple market adjustments and possible instability was avoided.† The system might be more efficient than a full market system, once the aspect of stability was accounted.

---

* Rader, "Pairwise Optimality and Non-competitive Behavior," in Quirk and Zarley, eds., *Papers in Quantitative Economics*, Vol. I, University of Kansas Press, Lawrence, Kansas, 1968.

† At this time, the degree of instability of multiple market systems is not completely solved. Many are stable (Arrow and Hurwicz, "On the Stability of the Competitive Equilibrium," "*Econometrica*, 26, 522–552, 1958), but instabilities may arise when there are complementarities between goods (Scarf, "Some Examples of Global Instability of the Competitive Equilibrium," *International Economic Review*, L, 157–172, (1960). Complementarities arise between land and labor in the agricultural sector and between capital and labor in the urban sector (Rader, "Normally Factor Inputs are Never Gross Substitutes," *Journal of Political Economy*, February, 1968. However, they do not impair stability (Rader, Chapter 7 of *Theory of General Economic Equilibrium*, forthcoming, Academic Press). Nevertheless complementarities may arise between goods on the consumer side and the stability of pure competition in such cases is not known.

Extra capital in agriculture could be transferred to the towns. Extra labor on land could be substituted for capital or labor, useful to the towns. Extra capital in the cities could be substituted for labor to send to the manors. Hence, production was factor connected. Since land was fixed, and in the case of capital saturation, whether or not agricultural labor obtained the same wage as rural labor, agricultural labor costs in rural wage rates was minimized so long as the relative wages of different kinds of labor was everywhere the same. Only if there were opportunities for investment in agriculture would equality of wage levels be necessary, for only in this case would comparisons between relative wages of capital and labor be important. (Lords had at least the same investment opportunities as the bourgeoisie and certainly bore the same rent on capital and probably the same rent on land.) In those areas without capital saturation, early in the feudal period, especially on the frontier, the manorial system was less important than were the free peasants, partially sponsored by capitalists of various sorts. Here the wage rates and returns to capital were competitive with the towns, again fulfilling the conditions sufficient for producer efficiency. Unemployment of factors was unknown in the countryside and rare in the towns, although possibly not in the capitalistic textile industries and in commerce.

The technological and educational industries were largely in the hands of the church. It is difficult to know exactly what the wages were, but in view of the fact that individuals freely entered the church's service, it would appear that material plus "psychic" income was up to the standards of the outside. Of course, incomes were provided by the church and its benefactors according to non-economic principles so that it is difficult to know if the marginal rates of substitution were equalized. However, it would seem that if there were excessive capital or land relative to other industrial opportunities, the church would invest in other enterprises, use the proceeds to hire labor, and increase its "output". Contrariwise, with too much labor, the church would do better to use the labor in secular work and acquire the needed capital. Obviously, the church did participate in extensive non-religious economic activities and it is hard to believe that there were any producer inefficiencies due to its manner of operation. In defence, the lords likewise had to acquire capital and labor at the urban market rates.

From the viewpoint of consumers, it is reasonable to assume that although there were differences of taxes, there was basic agreement upon what constituted goods. This was true at least to the degree that the society could not be disjointed into two groups with no goods in common. Even without similarity of tastes, the means of production were such as would occur only if some consumers did not consume the only goods (luxuries) another held desirable. Here, the means of production were such as to applicable to capital and/or land to yield the desired goods.

In conclusion from the producer viewpoint, Feudalism appears to have been in its time as efficient or more efficient than capitalism would have been.

9 REMARK

In time of full employment of capitalistic enterprises and saturation of capital in agriculture, Feudalism as described was producer efficient.

Assume a convex output set. To show that Feudalism was consumer efficient, one need only show that the prices which producers took as given were the same as consumer prices. Monopoly is an obvious counter instance. Otherwise, producers tried to maximize profits. However, discrepancies between urban and rural wages would lead to a different ratio of price to marginal costs in the towns and on the farms. Predictably, the interference of the state at the side of lords can be a source of consumer inefficiency, just as in the present day the interference of the state is usually clumsy and contrary to conditions of consumer prices proportional to producer prices proportional to marginal factor costs.

10 REMARK

Without monopoly and with equal urban and rural wages, Feudalism as described is consumer efficient. As shall be seen, equal urban and rural wages are most likely in the latter stages of feudalism.

In cases where Feudalism was not consumer efficient, it certainly was not distributively just. Otherwise, the position of the lords was due to military force, legal coercion and deception. So long as its adversaries were a weak willed and myopic peasantry, ever ready to compromise future years and future descendents for current benefits, the injustice was probably small—at least so far as the peasantry expression of self interest was concerned.* On the other hand, with growth of the bourgeosie and their recurrent disposession by the robber—knights and overbearing lords, a powerful and dangerous class harboured resentment of the great injustice. Tradesmen, manufacturers, and merchants together with the peasants and more progressive lords,

---

* In these neo-Calvinist days of Social Security and compulsary education, it is commonly thought that the lower class does not properly express in the market place its true interests, and by this judgement, Feudalism like all previous social systems was grossly injust.

were worse off than they would have been if the other lords with their lands and horses were wiped off the face of the earth. Consequently, they showed fear, respect, but no love for the great lords of the manors. In France, and England, they supported the Reformation and the Crown; in the low countries and Switzerland, they whittled away the lords' power. Only in Germany, outside the main cities, did the ancient lords hold their power, but here perhaps they held fast because West Germany was not so greatly feudalized and the grievances not so deep.

It is possible that Feudalism gained its bad name from the bourgeosie. Dark, backward, inefficient, it was reputed to be. These qualities it most emphatically did not display. Instead it was relatively productive, intelligent, enlightened, brutal and repressive. It was a not inappropriate system to reconcile relatively quick technical progress and the political fact of a dominant military.

ANALYSIS

1 MARKET FOR GOODS

Of those agricultural goods exported to the towns, some are used as raw materials in the manufacture of urban goods and services and others are directly consumed by the urban populace. Except for wages below the malnutrition margin, the demand for food and other agricultural products is highly inelastic. As real wages fall, the budget is dominated by agricultural goods and the elasticity of demand falls to perhaps one.

If Q^2 is urban output and β^{21} is the input-output matrix relating the urban requirements to rural goods, total urban demand is

$$c + \beta^{21}Q^2,$$

where c is the consumption of agricultural goods mainly by urban labor.
Possible shapes of the consumption function are illustrated in Figure 1.

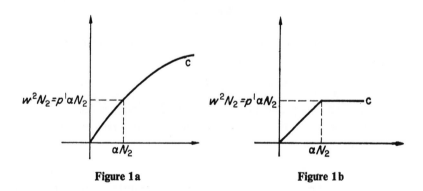

Figure 1a   **Figure 1b**

In the case of Figure 1b, up to wages equal to α, only a subsistence is demanded and thereafter only other commodities are purchased.

Given N_2, the demand curves of agricultural goods by the cities are illustrated in Figures 2a and 2b, for the cases in Figures 1a and 1b, respectively.

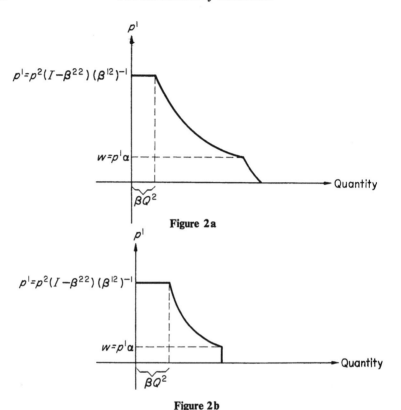

$$p^1 = p^2(I - \beta^{22})(\beta^{12})^{-1}$$

$$w = p^1\alpha$$

Quantity

$$\beta Q^2$$

Figure 2a

$$p^1 = p^2(I - \beta^{22})(\beta^{12})^{-1}$$

$$w = p^1\alpha$$

Quantity

$$\beta Q^2$$

Figure 2b

If β^{22} is the matrix of urban goods used to produce urban goods, value added in urban industries is given by

$$v^2 = p^2 - p^2\beta^{22} - p^1\beta^{12}.$$

If $v^2 = 0$, then wages and profits are zero. The income devoted to agricultural goods is constant for high prices where real wages are in excess of the malnutrition boundary,

$$w > p\alpha,$$

where α is the least cost vector of per capita consumption which yields zero rural population growth. Whenever price is less than that which gives malnutrition boundary, the demand curve is a displaced rectangular hyperbola. For lower prices it drops very steeply.

In agriculture, supply must equal demand.

$$(v + (1 - t)\lambda)Q^1 = c(wN_2, p^1) + \beta Q^{2'} \tag{1}$$

In Figure 3, equilibrium is at $\bar{p}^1$ and $\bar{Q}^1$.

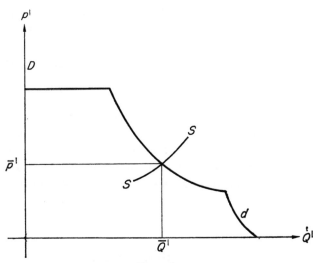

Figure 3

The upward slope of supply is due to the fact that there is a change in the proportion, t, which rural laborers spend their income on urban goods. Otherwise, the supply curve would be vertical given factors of production in agriculture. In more complicated cases where there are more than one good, there may be a shift in the composition of agricultural goods away from goods with relatively large inputs of more expensive urban goods. Since the quantity of urban goods used as inputs in agriculture production was small, this effect would not be important.

Reductions in agricultural supply lead to a rise in price in order to partially restore agricultural output to former levels and allow the urban factors to be fully employed.

1   REMARK

If agricultural demand is elastic, the net result of a decrease in agricultural output with fixed urban prices is a smaller flow of urban goods to the countryside. Otherwise, there is a larger outflow of urban goods.

Proof   In the elastic case, by definition price rises less than proportionately to quantity and the rural areas receive less in total value. Given the prices of urban goods, total urban goods purchased fall. The argument for the inelastic case proceeds in the obvious way.

q.e.d.

Since consumers use their increased income to increase their demands for urban goods, there will be differential effects on the prices of urban goods. Hence, some changes in the prices of various urban goods may be forthcoming. If urban and rural demands are such that increases in the price of one good increase the demand for others, it is said that goods are *gross substitutes*. If goods are gross substitutes, a reduction in the supply of agricultural goods will lead to an increase in the relative price of agricultural goods *vis a vis* urban goods.* Therefore, agriculture will be in a more favorable position provided the increases in price leads to a more than proportional decrease in quantity, as it will in the inelastic case. As shall be seen, the lords will in some cases wish to increase agricultural output and in other cases, decrease it. Which is best depends mainly upon the elasticity of demand for agricultural goods.

2 THE POPULATION LOCI

A contrast between short run and long run optimization appears in the graphs of population choice available to the lords. In Figure 4, there is illustrated the short run choices at different levels of total population. The line E represents equi-population combinations of N_1 and N_2. There are infinite number of these lines, representing each possible total population. At some point on such a line, there is the short run optimal urban-rural population combination. The locus of these combinations leads to a function

$$N_2 = S(N_1).$$

N_1 represents the point at which rural wages are at the subsistence level. The point $\overline{N}_2$ is that beyond which the urban capital share grows sufficiently fast that further increases in urban labor tend to decrease labor income, if indeed there ever is such a point. The fall in labor income would offset the increased demand for rural goods from urban output. Therefore, it will pay the lords to increase N_2 and decrease N_1 up until the point where either

1) raw material demands exhaust the agricultural surplus so that real wages are zero and $p^1\beta^{12} = p^2(I - \beta^{22})$, or
2) total real income to the urban working class falls sufficiently fast to overcome the increased demand for raw materials.

---

* Hicks, *Value and Capital*, appendix, 1938, Oxford, and Morishima, *Equilibrium, Stability and Growth*.

In the first case, for large enough N_1 the workers consume virtually no urban goods,

$$\lambda Q^1 = \beta^{12} Q^2,$$

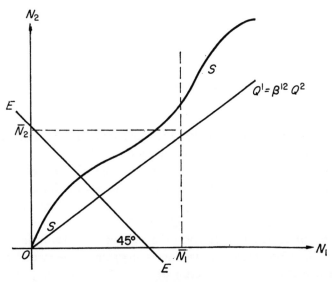

Figure 4

Clearly, in this equation, a larger N_1 allows a larger N_2, since increases in N_1 increase land income, λQ^1, and allow an increase in urban output.

In the second case, $N_2 > \overline{N}_2$, as illustrated in Figure 3. The slope of the curve, S, can be shown to be large as N_1 tends to zero. To see this, consider any finite ratio of N_2 to N_1. As N_2 and Q^2 both tend to zero, labor in each industry tends to zero, and the average output, g_i/N_2, for industry i tends to the ratio of the marginals, or

$$\frac{gi}{N_2} \to \frac{g_{N_2^i}}{1} \to \infty.$$

2   REMARK

As N_2 and Q_2 tend to zero, food demands from the industry's workers are outweighed by raw materials demands and the ratio of raw materials demand to total demand for agricultural goods tends to one. Also, on $S(N_1)$, agricultural prices tend to their maximum

$$p^1 \beta^{12} = p^2 (I - \beta^{22})$$

8*

Proof Let $c^i(w, p)$ be rural consumption by workers in the given industry.

$$\frac{\beta_j^i g^i}{\beta_j^i g_i + c_j^i(w/p)} = \frac{1}{1 + \dfrac{c_j^i(w,p)}{\beta_j^i g_i}} \to 1$$

since

$$\frac{c_j^i(w,p)}{\beta_j^i g_i} \leqq \frac{\alpha_j N_2^i}{\beta_j^i g_i} \to 0.$$

Rural demand tends to zero relative to raw materials. Therefore raw materials eventually exhaust the supply of rural goods.

To show that urban wages are bounded in terms of urban goods, assume the contrary. By remark 1, for high urban wages the lords wish to decrease N_1 to lower urban prices, provided the effect on the land share is not too deleterious. By remark 1 of Chapter 3, *assuming the rural elasticities of substitution do not tend to zero*, the relative decrease in land share is bounded. Therefore, there are ever increasing gains to be made by decreasing N_1 and increasing N_2. (In terms of figure 3, the economy is operating in the very inelastic portion of the agricultural demand curve). The lords therefore seek to decrease N_1 and increase N_2 contrary to $N_2 \to 0$.

The urban wages are bounded but the marginal product of rural labor tends to infinity. Therefore in each industry, urban value added must tend to zero.

In the long run, the lords must account for the fact that puting too much labor into the non-agricultural sector may cause total population to decline. That is to say, the lords must plan upon observing the constraint of population equilibrium. Therefore N_2 is a function of N_1 given by

$$\frac{dN}{dt} = n_1 N_1 + n N_2 = 0$$

or

$$N_2 = L(N_1).$$

The long run labor equilibrium combinations are shown in Figure 5 below, where $N_2 = L(N_1)$ is the urban labor force required to sustain a given N_1.

(At $\overline{N}_1$, urban wages are equal to α).

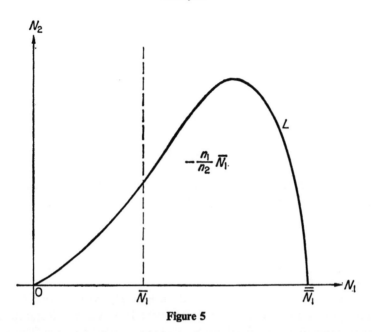

Figure 5

Intuitively, for each N_2 there are two ways in which population can be stabilized, first, by having a large rural population with a small (positive) rural birth rate and second, by having a small rural population with a large rural birth rate.

3 REMARK

Very small urban populations must be associated with very small rural populations. This is due to the fact that the urban death rate would tend to infinity if urban population remained greater than zero as rural population, and therefore agricultural surplus tended to zero. Obviously, an infinite death rate would require not a zero level of agricultural labor, but a large level to provide enough population to overcome the high death rate in the cities.

Alternatively, $\overline{N}_1$ such that rural wages are at the subsistence level is also compatible with a zero level of urban labor.

It will also be shown that the slope of L is finite at $N_1 = 0$. Clearly, for agricultural labor less than that giving the malnutrition wage

$$N_1 < \overline{N}_1,$$

$$\frac{dN_1 n_1}{dN_1} = n_1.$$

Proof As

$$N_1 \to 0,$$

$$\beta^{12} Q^2(N_2, K) \leqq Q^1$$

$$Q^1 \to 0, \text{ so that}$$

$$Q^2 \to 0$$

and therefore,

$$N_2 \to 0. \qquad\qquad \text{q.e.d.}$$

The urban death rate is at least $-n_2$. Therefore, a unit change in N_2 must be matched by at least $-(n_1/n_2)$ of N, i.e.

$$\frac{dL}{dN_1} < -\frac{n_1}{n_2}$$

This is illustrated in Figure 5.

Symmetrically, one might think that for each N_1 there are two N_2 which meet the population and market requirements. However, this is not the case. Every increase in N_2, N_1 fixed, leads to a lower real urban wage. The reason for this is that an increase in urban labor increases urban output and therefore increases the demand for raw materials. Since the agricultural surplus is fixed, there must be a smaller quantity of agricultural goods available to a larger agricultural labor force. Therefore, the real wages fall and the rate of reproduction falls. Since total urban reproduction was already negative, total reproduction falls.

4 REMARK

$$\frac{\partial n_2 N_2}{\partial N_2} = n_2 + \frac{\partial n_2}{\partial N_2} N_2$$

is always negative, $n_2 N_2$ is monotonic decreasing in N_2, and therefore there is at most on N_2 for which

$$n_2 N_2 = n_1 N_1.$$

It is easy find where the slope of L is positive:

5 REMARK

$$\frac{dL}{dN_1} > 0$$

whenever the rural reproduction rate, n_1, is a constant, i.e. whenever rural wages exceed the malnutrition level, α, and even beyond.

Proof An increase in rural labor leads to an increase in the agricultural surplus. Therefore, either the demand for agricultural goods for use as raw materials must be appropriately increased, which requires an increase in N_2, or else the demand for agricultural goods for urban labor consumption increases. If urban labor is already paid more than the malnutrition level, the only way to increase sufficiently the demand by urban labor is to increase the quantity of urban labor, N_2. Very great increases in urban wages could not result from increases in N_1 simply because the workers would spend the larger part of their wages on urban goods which would occur only if their marginal products increased which would occur only if N_2 greatly decreased. The net effect would be to reduce, not increase, agricultural demand.

Otherwise, one can greatly increase the demand either by increasing the quantity of urban labor or by increasing the real urban wage rate. Two subcases arise. First, so long as agricultural population growth is positively related to total agricultural population,

$$\frac{dn_1 N_1}{dN_1} > 0,$$

a decrease in urban labor together with an increase in the real urban wage rate decreases deaths in the cities and requires a cutback in N_1. Therefore, the rate of change of N_2 with respect to N_1 is positive,

$$\frac{dL}{dN_1} > 0,$$

so long as

$$\frac{dn_1 N_1}{dN_1} > 0.$$

In particular, so long as agricultural labor is less than that giving the maluntrition wage, $N_1 < \overline{N}_1$, the slope of L is positive.

Second, there is the case where rural wages are above real urban wages which in the feudal regime is a very unlikely eveets. (Case one and case two are not mutually exclusive but each does cover situations the other does not). The decrease in deaths from a decrease in N_2 (and a higher real urban wage rate) exceeds any decrease in deaths from a corresponding decrease in N_1. Therefore, population equilibrium could not be maintained unless N_1 were cut quite drastically, which would reduce the agricultural surplus to a level too low to cover demand.

q.e.d.

3 URBAN AND RURAL WAGES

Given the free labor in the towns, it is very difficult for the lords to keep the rural wage above the urban one. Individual lords, serfs, and farmers would be tempted to import the labor from the towns and labor would be happy to oblige. In Table 1, it is seen that in England, 1261–1400, the wages of thatchers are about 80% of those of a carpenter. Assume that the carpenter spends 10 years in apprenticeship or as a journeyman, while the thatcher needs only 5 years experience. The working life of a laborer is 35 years. Then the differential could well be payment for the extra 5 years training. The thatcher's wage is smaller relative to that of the mason—possibly because the mason's required a higher level of skill than the carpenter (assuming relatively low rates of interest.) Hence, there is no reason to believe there were significant wage differentials between town and country— except possibly to account for cost of living.* The very existence of free agricultural labor would lead one to suspect an equalization of rural and urban wage rates.

It is still possible for the serf to receive less for his work than free labor. It will appear that a great divergence would be contrary to the interests o the lords, both short term and long term. This fact rationalizes the existence of a free rural labor force.

The argument is straightforward. Should urban labor receive a wage above the malnutrition boundary, the demand for agricultural goods is likely to be highly inelastic. By driving labor out of agriculture, the supply of urban goods relative to rural goods will increase and the rural areas will benefit. Since the lords have the largest share of urban goods, they will benefit unless the decrease in labor supply reduces their share of agricultural output—a highly unlikely case in view of the fact that elasticities of substitution in agriculture would not exceed unity.

---

* Rogers, *op. cit.*, Chs. XV, XXIX.

Table 2 Rural/urban wages in England, 1261–1400

	Thatcher / Carpenter	Thatcher / Mason
1261–1270	.64	.80
1271–1280	.95	—
1281–1290	.61	.54
1291–1300	.95	.91
1301–1320	.83	.63
1311–1320	.78	.72
1321–1330	.88	.80
1331–1340	.88	.78
1341–1350	.92	.82
1351–1360	.82	.72
1361–1370	.78	.65
1371–1380	.82	.67
1381–1390	.81	.64
1391–1400	.90	.73

Source: J. E. T. Rogers, *A History of Agriculture and Prices in England*, 1259–1400.

6 THEOREM

If the elasticities of substitution in agriculture are less than or equal to one and the demand for rural goods is inelastic, it is in the short run interest of the lords to release serfs to the towns.

The theorem implies an urban wage below the malnutrition boundary where demands are elastic. Due to the great death rates in the city, serfs and peasant farmers would have to have wages in excess of the subsistence level. Hence, agricultural labor cannot receive a return much below urban labor.

The case for equalization of urban and rural wages is even stronger for long run optimization. As urban labor tends to zero, rural labor fixed, urban output tends to zero as does the demand for rural goods, both for consumption and raw materials. Hence, the price of agricultural goods tends to zero as does the lords income in terms of urban purchasing power.

7 THEOREM

Ordinarily, increases in labor decrease labor income. If so, whenever

$$N_2 = L(N_1) \text{ is decreasing in } N_1,$$

agricultural prices and urban output are decreasing, and eventually land income in urban prices is falling. If rural wages are below the malnutrition *boundary, it is never in the long run interests of the lords to allow, N_1, such that*

$$\frac{dL}{dN_1} \leqq 0.$$

Proof Population equilibrium requires that at a virtually zero urban reproduction rate there be a virtually zero urban population. So long as agricultural prices are increasing with increasing N_2, demand for agricultural goods increases either consumption by urban labor or raw materials demands. In the former case, with rising agricultural prices, urban labor must attain an increasing income, which is possible with fixed capital only if urban labor is increasing in supply. In the latter case, raw material demands can increase only if urban output increases and only if urban labor increases. Whenever increases in rural population decrease urban population, the reduced demand for agricultural goods lowers the income of the lords. So long as the wages in agriculture are below the malnutrition boundary, virtually all urban goods going to the countryside accrue to the lords. Since fewer urban goods are manufactured while the prices of urban goods are raised and the marginal product of urban capital increases, capitalists receive more and the lords less of urban manufactures.

q.e.d.

As before, if rural wages are below the malnutrition boundary, they must not be too far below, whereupon the margin between urban and rural wages is limited. It will be seen that as capital accumulates, there is a tendency toward complete equalization of wages between urban and rural sectors.

Between regions, say between different parts of England, France, the Low Countries, Germany, Spain, and Italy, there will be trade and some specialization. If inter-regional trade is free, there will be a tendency to so-called factor price equalization. Presumably capital-labor ratios will be similar between different towns and capital-labor and land-labor ratios will be similar between different rural areas. Since the number of industries exceeds the number of factors, small differences in factors can be accomodated without international differences in factor prices.* The factors can be employed simply by lowering different intensities of operation of industries.

---

* For an extension of the Hecksher-Ohlin factor price equalization theorem, see Rader, "International Trade and Development in a Small Country," in Quirk & Zarley, eds., *Papers in Quantitative Economics*, U. of Kansas Press, 1968.

This assumes transportation costs to be negligible which is regarded as a good approximation by Rogers.*

For example, a town with a relatively laɪge quantity of capital would specialize partially in capital intensive industries. Provided some town produced at least some of each good and provided other towns had similar but not necessarily identical factor endowments, there would be complete equalization of factor wages without any immigration. Beginning without greatly similar capital-labor ratios, capital would tend to move abroad to its higher return and effect equalization of capital returns. Somewhat short of complete equality of capital-labor ratios, there would be complete equality of factor wages and no further reason for international capital movements.

In the same way, the case for equalization of rates of return in agriculture was strengthened by the great migrations in the middle ages which would have tended to bring land-labor ratios closer together. Hence, the preoccupation with the dichotomy between urban and rural would be appropriate for the feudal economy since differences in factor wages would occur most often between the two and not between different countries.

An instance is afforded by efforts of the English crown to develop a textile industry.† Export taxes on wool were a source of revenue and the king tried to attract Flemish cloth makers to increase the value upon which the tax was levied. After subsidies were removed, the clothing industry gradually declined. The crown found it hard to prevent import of continental cloth and impossible to sustain an inappropriate industry. Economic and political conditions mitigated against protectionism and toward free trade, and in these circumstances there was no gain to equalizing factor endowments.

4 DYNAMICS WITHOUT CAPITAL ACCUMULATION

For long run optimization, there are no dynamics without capital accumulation. There is simply the lords' best point in population equilibrium. For short run optimization, there is a more variegated dynamical theory which is presented in preparation for and in contrast to the accumulative case.

To analyze the path of the economic variables over time whenever the class of lords are optimizers in the short run, consider first the course of population changes in the absense of the accumulation of capital.

---

* Rogers, *op. cit.*
† E. Lipson, *The History of the Woolen and Worsted Industries*, A. C. Bloch, London, 1921, Ch. III.

Figure 5 is reproduced in Figure 6. Whenever (N_1, N_2) are above the locus, N_2 exceeds the stationary level so that net total population is decreasing. Of course, rural population will be increasing so that the movement is

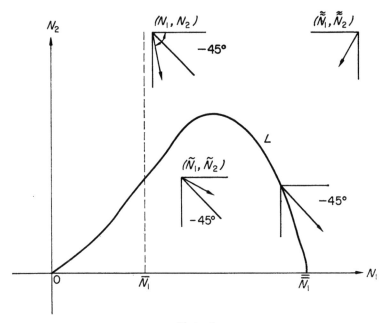

Figure 6

toward greater N_1 and less N_2, but at an angle more than $-45°$, as illustrated by the arrow in Figure 6. If N_1 and N_2 are large enough, both decline $((\tilde{N}_1, \tilde{N}_2)$ in Figure 6). Of course, the points on the graph of $L(N_1)$ are not of themselves stable, and in fact movement takes place from them at a $-45°$ angle. Only at $(\overline{\overline{N}}_1, 0)$ is there no tendency for population change in the absence of manipulation by the lords. Below the graph of $L(N_1)$, N_1 is too large so that there is a net growth in population. Still urban population is is declining and therefore the movement from $(\tilde{N}_1, \tilde{N}_2)$ is downward and to the right, but at an angle less than $-45°$, as illustrated by the arrow in Figure 6.

To add the lords as a short run optimizing class, consider that they adjust N_2 and N_1 so as to increase u. This is illustrated in Figure 7, which is Figure 3 super imposed on Figure 4. Above the locus, S, of (N_1, N_2) for which $(\partial u/\partial N_1) - (\partial u/\partial N_2) = 0$, the lords seek to increase the rural labor force and decrease the urban labor force. Below S, they seek to increase the urban labor force and decrease the rural labor force. The efforts of the lords are in addition to and without consideration of the natural population forces illustrated in Figure 6. Therefore, the net effect is the resolution of the two. An equilibrium on the locus of population combination would be reached

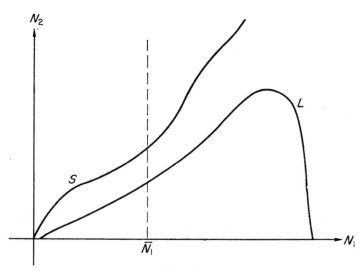

Figure 7

only if the lords' efforts just offset the natural forces. This would be the case where the direction of the lords' changes were at a 45° angle and of the same magnitude as the natural population change. In particular, such an equilibrium would have to be on $L(N_1)$. Normally, the optimizing direction of change will be variable and it is likely that some where on $L(N_1)$, there will be exactly a 45° angle between the natural population change and the optimizing population change initiated by the lords. But the magnitude of population change is dependent upon the power of the lords, and the coincidence of the magnitude and directions of the two sources of population change would appear to be very accidental.

8 REMARK

Normally the system has no overall equilibrium of population forces.

Nevertheless, the population combinations will stay bounded. As N_2 becomes very large, population decreases due to the natural causes predominate and the large N_2 is not sustained. As N_1 becomes very large, starvation appears in the countryside and therefore N_1 falls as well. Consequently, one can apply a powerful result of ordinary differential equations, namely the Poincare-Bendixsen theorem, to conclude the following.

9 REMARK

Population tends to a cycle, as time increases. This is illustrated in Figure 8. Along the cycle C, beginning at (N_1, N_2), the lords change the natural direction of slightly Southeast to Southwest. This continues as the direction

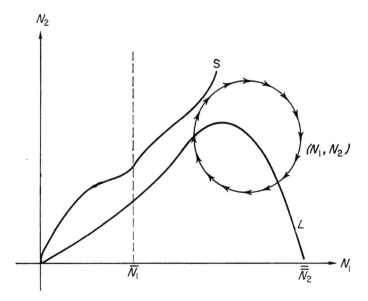

Figure 8

slowly becomes that due to the natural laws, since the lords are moving closer to their optimum and are therefore less willing to expend resources on population changes. Eventually, the system moves far from an optimum and the lords begin to act again. Points not on C may tend to C, as in Figure 9.

If there are several cycles, the movement may be more complicated for paths not beginning on the cycles.

If the accident of intersection of the two curves L and S does not occur, then the system does not stay long in the region above S. If population were above $S(L_1)$, the lords and reproduction would be working together to move out of the region. Therefore. the history of the system would be such that most of the time the lords would send labor to the cities.

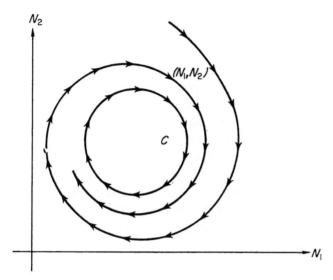

Figure 9

5 THE POPULATION EQUATION UNDER CAPITAL ACCUMULATION

There is little evidence on the accumulation of capital per capital in the Middle Ages. What there is indicates a steady growth. First, many cathedrals and town buildings and walls were constructed during the period. Whether or not these were built in excess of normal population growth would be hard to ascertain. The medieval custom of accounting population by number of churches might suggest a constant ratio of buildings to populations.* On the other hand, it is possible that authorities changed the ratio appropriate to increasing wealth.

Second, as remarked in Chapter 3, many of the technical improvements in urban production were capital intensive, indicative of an increasing capital-labor ratio.

Third, there was developed an extensive banking system concentrated in Flanders, North Italy and South Germany.† Such a "capital market" could be indicative of events other than an increase in the capital labor ratio. Increases in the scale of commerce might bring the scale of financial trans-

---

* Williams, *op. cit.*

† Richard Ehrenberg, *Capital and Finance in the Age of the Renaissance*, translated by H. M. Lucas, Augustus M. Kelly, 1963, 1963, New York, "Introduction."

actions to the level at which formal banking could facilitate capital movements. Population increases alone could lead to such a market. The evidence for increased commerce and population is great, both from reports of the time and archeological remains.* Also, differential capital accumulation between classes could have the same effect. Many feudal businesses operated with capital borrowed from the wealthy.† Possibly there were similar transfers on an international scale. For example, if the resident of one country saved whereas those of another dissaved, a capital market would facilitate the transfer of capital from the one area to the other. No net change in the capital-labor ratio would be required. Differential rates of saving would require capital movements only after it had advanced to the stage where certain towns were forced to the point of complete specialization in labor intensive goods. Hence, the capital market might develop only late in the history of Feudalism.

Fourth, it is possible that the gradual erosion of the ecclesiastical ban on usury was conducive to greater savings. Equally well, it is possible that the development of a formal capital market was merely the realization of legitimacy for an already viable system.

The best evidence for growth in the capital labor ratio would be the labor saving innovations. The growth of a capital market is supporting evidence if it served manufacturers as well as traders. (Only a small amount of capital could be absorbed by expanding per capital trade which would accompany an increased geographical specialization of production).

Hereafter, it is presumed that the early history of feudalism was that associated with a small capital stock, whereas its late history was associated with a much larger one.

10 REMARK

L must shift down as urban capital accumulates.

Proof Suppose N_2 associated with a given N_1 does not decrease. An increase in the productivity of the urban areas leads to an increase in the industrial demand for agricultural goods. Given the agricultural output, agricultural prices must rise. The equilibration is done at the expense of urban labor, since in the end, urban output must be higher than before, which takes a greater proportion of the unchanged agricultural output for use as raw materials. The urban workers are left with fewer goods (and real

---

* Pirrenne, Medieval cities: *Their Origin and the Revival of Trade*, Princeton, 1925).

† Postan, "Credit in Medieval Trade, "*Economic History Review*, I., 1928.

income). As capital accumulates, given N_1 and N_2, urban laborers find their real wages reduced by the amount of increase in the demand for rural raw materials, resulting from the increase in urban production capital. Therefore, given N_1, only a smaller N_2 is compatible with population equilibrium.

q.e.d.

In order to ascertain the overall trends, it is necessary to know both from where the system is coming and to where the system is going. Therefore, attention is paid to both cases, a zero capital stock and a maximum capital stock.

For small capital stocks, it is in the interest of the lords to maintain the urban labor force at some minimum level. As capital decreases, the fall in urban product places a premium on restoring urban output to its former level. This can never be fully accomplished since otherwise the labor force would quickly exceed that which could be fed by the agricultural surplus and the number of deaths would become so large as to violate the requirement of population equilibrium. On the other hand, suppose N_2 tended to zero without N_1 tending to the subsistence level. Death rates would have to rise to absorb the given growth of population in the countryside, whereupon real urban wages would have to fall to zero. Since the marginal product of urban labor is rising, agricultural prices would then rise to the point where agriculture obtained all the urban output. However, instead agricultural prices tend to zero since a rapidly falling urban demand for rural good is "chasing" a finite rural supply. As will be seen, when given the choice between a large urban output or a large rural output, the lords will choose the former, at least before driving rural labor to the subsistence level.

11 REMARK

At very low capital stocks, where urban output is very small, given the level of agricultural labor, there is a minimum (non-zero) quantity of urban labor.

At first, capital decumulation will force a shift to capital intensive goods which decreases the capital share. However, if the urban elasticities of substitution are less than one, the (urban) capitalist share of a given urban good tends to zero as the capital/labor ratio tends to zero. In the limit whatever goods finally predominate the share of urban laborers in the urban output tends to one.

12 REMARK

At very low capital stocks, real urban wages tend to the malnutrition level or less. They do not fall to zero, and virtually all urban goods go to agriculture.

Proof If urban wages remain more than some $\varepsilon > 0$ above the malnutrition level, the share of urban labor in output would be an unnecessary drain from the lords. With N_2 bounded from zero, urban wages tending to zero would contradict the population equilibrium equations. Also, the agricultural surplus is eventually dominated by demands by urban workers, i.e. the value of the surplus tends to the value of worker's income. Since worker income as a proportion of urban income tends to one, the value of the agricultural surplus as a proportion of urban income tends to one.

q.e.d.

Let capital accumulate indefinitely. *Given agricultural population*, urban population, N_2, must tend to zero. The urban wages cannot exceed the malnutrition wages, since in that case a zero urban labor force would have a zero death rate and therefore population equilibrium would require $N_1 = \bar{N}_1$ or $N_2 = 0$. The fact of bounded wages implies that urban wages must tend to zero. Since marginal product of labor tends to infinity, value added tends to zero, and the cost of raw materials must eventually exhaust urban output.

13 REMARK

As capital increases indefinitely, urban wages tend to zero. The agricultural sector captures a larger and larger proportion of the urban output. Also, urban output has a finite, non-zero limit equal to $Q^1(\beta^{21})^{-1}$. After urban wages fall to the level of rural wages, there is equality of wages and ultimately a falling urban population. The above results applied to N_1:

14 REMARK

For large capital stocks, urban wages are below rural wages at N_1, and therefore dL/dN_1 remains positive for some time afterwards. For small capital stocks, rural wages are nearly equal to or else below the malnutrition level so that again dL/dN_1 remains positive, but possibly for a somewhat shorter period. The results may not hold at intermediate levels, depending upon how quickly the capital share rises as capital falls.

15 REMARK

For very low urban elasticities of substitution, the capital share rises very rapidly in response to a decrease in its quantity, and at $\bar{N}_1$, rural wages are again above the urban wages for all levels of capital stock.

16 REMARK

Given N_2, capital tends to infinity as it accumulates at a steady rate.

Proof If not, output would tend to zero, which implies that the raw material requirements tend to zero, or rural output tends to $\beta^{21}Q^2$ tends to zero which is impossible.

q.e.d.

6 DYNAMICS

Normally, the short run and long run optima will be disturbed as capital changes. The particular way depends upon the initial level of capital stock. Consider the case of short run optimization.

First, let capital tend to zero at a fixed labor distribution. Since the supply of agricultural goods remains fixed whereas urban demand falls to zero as urban output decreases, agricultural prices tend to zero. A decrease in agricultural surplus is able to substantially raise rural prices. On the other hand, an increase in urban demand will substantially raise rural prices as well. Therefore, an increase in rural labor at the expense of urban labor will increase the value of the surplus.

17 REMARK

At very low capital stocks where the agricultural wage rate is below the malnutrition level, where most accrues to the landowners, the short run optimizing change is that which decreases N_1 and increases N_2.

If the rural wage rate is above the malnutrition level, it pays the lords to increase urban labor only if the reduction in rural labor does not so decrease the land share as to reduce land income. If the land share is nearly constant, short run optimization is served by increasing N_2 and decreasing N_1 until the increases in urban prices from increases in N_2 are nearly zero, due to limited capital). If N_2 is sufficiently large that the reduction in the land share from a decrease in N_1 outweighs the increase due to increased agricultural prices, the lords will find it in their interests to reduce urban labor. As capital tends to zero, this case becomes more likely.

18 REMARK

Given N_1 and N_2, N_2 above $\bar{N}_2$, for a very small capital stock, and in the case where decreases in N_1 reduce the lords share of urban output by however little it pays the lords to reduce N_2 and increase N_1.

Remark 18 applies to a country such as Italy at the time of the Germanic conquests, where an oversupply of urban population not only dies off but is contrary to the interest of the lords, given that there have been agricultural innovations which raise agricultural output above the subsistence level. Of

9*

course, the reason the lords seek to populate the countryside is to reduce the labor share of urban output. In terms of Figure 8, Italy is a case where population begins above the optimizing locus. In contrast, for N_2 small relative to the capital stock, the lords will seek to increase the size of the cities even in the face of the fact that the peasants enjoy an above subsistence level of income.

At the other extreme, consider the case where capital increases indefinitely. Eventually, agricultural prices rise to the point where urban wages are zero, where $p^2(I - \beta^{22}) = p^1\beta^{12}$. The capital stock at which this price obtains represents the maximum capital stock compatible with a non-negative wage for urban factors. At this point all the agricultural surplus is used for raw materials, so that all urban output goes to the agricultural sector.

In the case where K is near but not equal to $\bar{K}$, where urban wages are zero, suppose the rural wage rate is below the malnutrition boundary. An increase in N_2 will increase the demand for raw materials. At large capital stock, urban wages will be high enough that consumption will be unresponsive to the decrease in urban real wages. The price of agricultural goods will rise. Virtually all the agricultural surplus accrues to the land owners and their position will improve.

19 REMARK
At high capital stocks, and large agricultural populations an increase in N_2 and a decrease in N_1 leads to an increase in the value of the land share.

The analysis for the case $t > 0$ follows as in the instance of $N_1 > \bar{N}_1$, except that the level of N_2 must be higher in order to induce the lords to decrease the size of the cities. In short, as capital accumulates, $L(S)$ shifts down.

At intermediate levels of agricultural population, where N_1 is near but less than $\bar{N}_1$, there may be a temporary fall in part of the locus, S, as illustrated in Figure 10. Note also that L shifts down (remark 10). This will undoubtedly affect the dynamic system, but it is very hard to see in what way.

20 THEOREM
For short run optimization under capital accumulation, the basic cyclical pattern would remain. There is no reason to expect an equilibrium of population forces to result as a consequence of the accumulation of capital until urban wages equal rural wages after which population distribution is determined by the equality of wages.

The intersection of the optimizing locus with the stable population locus is unlikely at any level of capital stock, and impossible for very large ones, since eventually S rises whereas L falls. The system will tend to operate below the optimizing locus and the short run optimizing lords will encourage the growth of the cities, especially at large capital stocks.

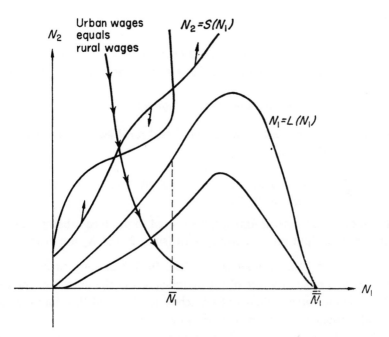

Figure 10

Technical change increases productivity without affecting much the factor shares. Technical change in agriculture merely sets the system back to a previous position since the quantity of urban goods per unit of agricultural surplus is reduced. Similarly, technical change in the cities sets the system forward.

For a class of lords who are long run maximizers, the dynamics are straight–forward. The lords place and keep population at a stationary level in keeping with their interests. Only as capital accumulates in the cities is there any change in the population of society. The locus, $L(N_1)$ shifts down (in Figure 10) as capital accumulates, but also the maximizing value of the land share, changes. Hence, one must again have recourse to a detailed analysis.

Let capital decrease to zero as in section 5.

21 THEOREM

As capital decumulates under long run optimization,

1) N_2 *remains bounded and above zero.*
2) $Q^2 \to 0$
3) $g_{N2}^i \to 0$ *for all i,*
4) $p^1 \to 0$
5) *the capital share of urban output tends to one,*
6) *real rural wages tend to a value somewhat greater than zero but not greater than* α,
7) *real value of urban output tends to infinity,*

until such time as real urban wages equal real rural wages after which time real wages tend to zero.

Proof First, rural wages are above the subsistence level. For N_1 near $\bar{N}_1$, N_2 must be very small. Therefore,

1) most of the agricultural surplus is used to produce urban goods, and
2) urban output must be nearly zero (since K and N_2 are nearly zero).

Clearly, 1) and 2) contradict each other. In fact as long as N_2 remains bounded, as it must by virtue of the boundedness of the growth of the agricultural labor force, urban output tends to zero and therefore the agricultural surplus used for raw materials must tend to zero.

If $N_2 \to 0$, increases in N_2 have an ever increasing effect on the demand for agricultural goods and therefore have an ever increasing effect on the price of agricultural goods. Decreases in N_1 will lower agriculture surplus and raise agricultural prices, but as rural wages exceed the malnutrition level, the share of land owners in agricultural surplus will gradually fall. This will eventually outweigh the increase in agricultural prices from decrease in demand. Also, decreases in N_1 eventually force decreases in N_2 in order to attain population equilibrium, which effect will ultimately be strong enough to actually raise agricultural prices. There will be a tendency for both agricultural and urban population to be somewhat greater than zero.

Considering $N_1 \geq \bar{N}_1$, any decrease in rural population will allow urban population to be increased without greatly changing the lord's share of urban output. Hence, so long as

$$\frac{dL}{dN_1} < 0,$$

it pays to increase urban labor at the expense of rural labor. Therefore, no N_1's giving agriculture a malnutrition wage are chosen by the lords.

q.e.d.

22 REMARK

At small capital stocks, the long run optimum occurs at an intermediate point, between 0 and $\bar{N}_1$, for which agricultural labor receives more than the malnutrition level.

Let capital be accumulated indefinitely, and recall again the analysis of section 4, for the case of given $N_1 \neq \bar{N}_1$, $N_1 \neq 0$.

23 THEOREM

As capital accumulates out of capitalists income,

1) $N_2 \to 0$,
2) *real rural wages* $\to 0$,
3) $K \to \infty$,
4) $p^1\beta^{12} \to p^2(I - \beta^{22})$
5) *capital share* $\to 0$
6) *the agricultural surplus* $\to$ *raw materials used in urban output*

until the equalization of urban and rural wages rates whereupon 1), 3), 5), *and* 6) *hold.*

Proof As N_2 tends to zero, the rate of change of prices to changes in N_1 becomes infinite due to the fact that a consequent change in N_2 yields an ever larger increase in the supply of urban goods which increases the demand for rural goods. Thus, the demand for rural goods rises indefinitely. It is this effect which ultimately dominates the considerations of the lords, and therefore, any given $N_1 < \bar{\bar{N}}_1$ eventually becomes short of the lords' long run optimum. As capital accumulates, N_1 increases to $\bar{\bar{N}}_1$, the point of zero rural population growth. Furthermore, in transit to this point the lords find it in their interest to transfer population to the cities and thereby encourage somewhat the growth of the cities.

Whatever the real wage rate, as $N_1 \to \bar{\bar{N}}_1$, $N_2 \to 0$, by virtue of theorem 18 of Chapter 1. Consequently, as capital accumulates out of capitalist profits, capital tends to infinity. If not, urban output tends to zero and therefore most of the agricultural surplus must go to urban labor, which is impossible since urban labor and its consumption of agricultural goods tend to zero. Indeed, raw materials costs must eventually exhaust urban output so that

$$p^1\beta^{12} \to p^2(I - \beta^{22}).$$

Real wages can be shown to tend to the malnutrition level or below, as agriculture gains a stronger hold on urban output. Anything short of malnutrition real urban wage would mean that urban labor obtained a definite share of urban output. It can be shown that this would not be in the lords' interest.

Indeed, one can show that urban wages tend to zero. Consider that urban output tends to the landowners' share or urban output.

Let N_1^n tend to N_1 and K^n be chosen large enough so that the associated wage tends to zero. Now the N_2^n associated with K^n leads to an optimizing output which is nearly equal to urban output at (N_2^n, K^n). The optimizing output may be a little larger to give more to the lords. It cannot be smaller due to a smaller N_2, since this would lead to a higher urban wage rate and a lower price for agricultural goods—never in the lords' interest. Therefore, the optimizing N_2 is at least as large as N_2^n and the urban wage rate is no larger than that associated with N_2^n.

q.e.d.

In summary, at a low capital stock, the long run optimum population allows a (possibly modest) excess for agricultural laboreres over the malnutrition level, and places the rural laboreres more or less at that level. Then as K increases (to infinity) the lords find it in their interests to increase population and allow migration to the cities even though they do not let them expand as much as it is possible. The cities can utilize the limited agricultural surplus with less and less labor to obtain more and more produce for the countryside. The lords "oblige" the towns by making the agricultural surplus as large as compatible with population equilibrium. But the lords extract an ever burdensome price for agricultural goods. As total population expands, real urban wages drop to the rates in rural areas which fall also, but merely to the subsistence level where total agricultural population growth is zero. The cities decline in population whereas the countryside grows. Of course, in the international market, there is a still stronger tendency to increase agricultural labor and depress agricultural wages, but with a faster decrease in urban population and therefore possibly a less rapid fall in real urban wages. Even areas without towns will compete with towns and there the lords will pursue policies of releasing labor to the towns and depressing the wages of urban workers to the rural levels.

The long run tendencies of the system will be delayed by increases in agricultural technology. If these technical innovations occur continuously, then total population will increase and urban population may increase as well, but will be a declining proportion of the total.

In both short run and long run optimization urban and rural wages fall and are eventually equalized. In both instances the "terms of trade" turn against the urban areas until wage equalization is attained. These conclusions would seem to provide tests for the political theory presented that states followed policies beneficial to the lords. The (rather strong) evidence for equal wages in the late feudal period has already been considered. It would be conclusive only if there were an excess of rural over urban wages in the earlier periods. The best information available is the rather late record of a free agricultural labor force and the gradual commutation of obligations of labor to obligations of money. The latter would be valid evidence only upon the assumptions that such commutations would occur only if they were in the interest of the individual lord. In Table 2, there does not seem to be a positive trend, which is consistent with an advanced state of per capita capital stock—accentuated by the plague but at a relatively high level even in the half century before.

If one could actually compute the income of villiens, a direct comparison of villien income with free laborer could be made. Unfortunately, the (average) income accruing to villiens is an unsolved problem in medieval economic history.

In Table 3, with much fluctuation, wool cloth to raw wool turned in favor of agriculture until the plague when it rose sharply. Afterwards, the terms of trade began to turn in favor of agriculture again. There is an obvious decline in the English wool market. This is most striking in the wool/wine price ratio, which was due in part to the devastation of supply in the Hundred Years War in France. It is possible that France was also a consumer of English wool as well as a major producer of wine which would give a double reason for the decline in the market. With regard to wool-steel and wool-linen there is little trend until long after the great plague whereupon the terms of trade turned *against* agriculture. For wheat, the terms of trade are more favorable and in the case of wheat/steel there is considerable improvement over time. Wheat/millstone and wheat/linen display a slight upward trend at first and then a slight downward trend whereas wheat/wine still goes against England and in favor of the continent. On the whole, the price predictions of the analysis would seem borne out.

In distinguishing between short run and long run optimization, the reaction of the English state at the time of the black death is informative. A shift in population was made which hit the rural and urban areas simultaneously wherever they were on the cycle. Such a disaster would not have altered the fact that the short run maximizing lords should have kept urban

Table 3 Rural/Urban Prices in England, 1261–1400

Date	best cloth	2nd quality cloth	wool	wool	wool	wool	wine	wine	wine	wheat*	wheat	wheat	wheat	wheat
	wool	wool	mill-stone	steel	linen	wine	mill-stone	steel	linen	wool	mill-stone	steel	linen	wine
1261–1270	100	100	100	100	100	100	100	100	100	100	100	100	100	100
1271–1280	—	84	98	107	91	138	71	78	66	118	115	126	107	162
1281–1290	102	104	94	104	195	136	69	76	143	110	104	115	214	150
1291–1300	90	123	62	81	118	94	66	86	126	148	92	120	175	139
1301–1310	—	87	79	122	133	52	152	235	256	119	94	145	158	62
1311–1320	106	81	83	111	135	58	143	191	231	152	126	164	203	88
1321–1330	64	77	99	118	129	52	171	227	249	143	142	153	168	63
1331–1340	—	81	72	96	98	35	206	274	280	124	89	119	122	42
1341–1350	79	108	88	93	82	16	550	590	511	148	130	138	121	23
1351–1360	122	147	46	68	60	20	230	325	300	204	97	137	122	42
1361–1370	—	—	53	89	49	24	220	370	204	150	79	133	73	36
1371–1380	110	160	48	115	62	27	177	426	230	105	50	121	65	38
1381–1390	—	—	47	78	60	23	205	338	260	124	58	97	74	29
1391–1400	89	47	48	96	73	54	89	178	172	124	60	119	90	67

* Great Wool

Source: Rogers, *A History of Agriculture and Prices in England, 1259–1400.*

population high and continued to contribute to its sustenance. The system would then grind on as before, although perhaps only after some temporary and ineffective panic measurers—such as the freezing of rural wages. In particular, they would concentrate on restoring a "balance" between cities and the countryside rather than upon increasing population (remark 18). Instead, over the next century or so after the black death, very little migration took place to the cities.* This means that agricultural population was maximized, which in turn maximized population growth and allowed optimum population to be reestablished. The position of the lords deteriorated temporarily, more than it would have, for example, had they enclosed the land. Evidently, instead of adopting the best short run policy, they met the emergency by a policy optimal in the long run. Of course, this was at the end of the feudal period and all characteristics may not have been as we have described. Nevertheless, it may indicate the inclination of the land owners who controlled political power.

Information on feudalism is too sketchy to allow a fitting to data of the structural equations here presented, and one must instead be content with examing the implications of the system. The differences between the short run and long run versions are listed:

1) When capital accumulates slowly in the cities, under short run optimization, the ratio of urban to rural population fluctuates around long term trend whereas under long run optimization it tends to the long term trend.

2) Under short run optimization, the support of the cities is less enthussastic at low capital stocks than at high ones, especially in those parts of the cycle where there is a relatively large urban population. On the other hand, under long run optimization, after an initial adjustment, there is consistent tendency to induce population increases, both urban and rural, in order to partially offset rising urban death rates. Therefore, under long run optimization, the support for increasing the population of the cities is less enthusiastic at high capital stocks than at low ones.

3) Under short run optimization, as capital increases rural wages need not tend to the subsistence level, as they do under long run optimization. The reaction to the black death refers only to 2).

* Postan, M., "Some Economic Evidence of Declining Population in the Lyter Middle Ages." *The Economic History Review*, 2nd series, vol. 2, (1950). For a contrary view, see W. L. Langer, "The Black Death." *The Scientific American* (February, 1964). A rejoinder appears in J. Hirschleifer, *Disastery and Recovery: The Black Death in Western Europe*, RAND Corp. Memorandum RM-47000-TAB, 1966.

CHAPTER 5

POST FEUDAL EUROPE

---

1 LATENT FEUDALISM

In chapters 3 and 4, a model of a dual economy, agricultural and urban, was presented with special regard for the effects of an increase in population and various social policies *vis a vis* the relase of labor from the countryside to the cities. It was shown the lords' interest was served by dismantling the bonds of labor as capital accumulated in the cities, although they would wish to dismantle the system very slowly. The reestablishment of feudalism in East Europe was rationalized.

Although there was a Marxian assumption that political power is the instrument of the upper class and that feudalism contained the seed of its own destruction, it is not the decline of the position of the upper classes under feudalism but rather the greater opportunity under an alternative system which motivated the dismantling of the system. The Marx–Dobb view of social motivation is the Pavlovian impulse–response theory. In contrast, the (economist's) view here is that of a sequence of marginal adjustments aimed at optimizing welfare of some group, not just of "satisficing," whatever that might mean.

It is worth considering the Pirenne thesis in the light of the position taken here. The cutting off of the Eastern trade routes may have been a result of feudalism instead of a cause. On the other hand, the Muslims' trade restrictions may have played an indirect role, by forcing Western lords to be cognizant of the growth of towns. Nevertheless, the manorial system would not be overthrown by this element alone. The accumulation of capital in the cities is the additional element needed to explain the demise of feudalism. Consequently, a pre-Protestant version of Weber's Protestant Ethic plays an essential role in feudalism's decline.

As wages are equated between the rural and urban sectors, the advantages of the manorial system are reduced. Only in the areas where there are virtually no towns did it pay the lords as a class to keep labor on the manors. Even then the return was quite small since at best they simply assured a high degree of labor participation by forbidding exceptional serfs from seeking their fortune at a time when they were not likely to greatly improve their position. Consequently, in most of Northwest Europe, villainage was replace by tenancy.*

In the latter days, the survival of feudal claims on serfs is an anachronism, not serving any great social purpose but objectional only to the most able and adventuresome. Nevertheless, the underlying power structure of feudallism could be at odds with economic reality. In West Europe, this was the case during the 15th century and this set the stage for a class war between the landed aristocracy and urban bourgeosie.

In the early 15th century, although political authority still rested with the lords, the economic distinctiveness of feudalism was eroded. Nevertheless, there was an alternative to the subtle decentralized exploitation of the feudal age, namely the exercize of the power to tax. However, to exercize this power effectively, it was necessary to rebuild the state along classical lines. The difficulty was that the dominant economic class was no longer the lords but rather the bourgeoisie.

The radical economic shift of position of the lords is in contrast to that of businessmen. All through the later Middle Ages, great princes and petty lords alike were in arears to merchants, manufacturers, and bankers.† As the debt grew, the lords could repudiate it by force and thereby lose the opportunity of borrowing again, or they could surrender their lands and grant monopolies in payment. They did both, but the fact that they were improvident required them to be careful in their dealings with the bourgeoisie. Clearly, they would have to return again to borrow. Only after the establishment of well organized states could be lords assure themselves the dominant position through taxation. However, in the meantime the bourgeoisie recognized the ultimate threat and they followed two policies. In Switzerland, the Low Countries, and in the Hanseatic League, the towns were strong enough to resist aristocratic governments and finally won their freedom. In England and France, they helped to elevate the crown above the aristocratic level, thereby loosening the connection between state and class, and reducing the aristocracy from a position of sovereignty to one of subservience to the "national" interests. The modern era became characterized by a shift of power to manufacturing and trade, whence it lost its feudal character on political as well as economic grounds. There is no need to prove this thesis since it is well enough documented in the historical literature.

---

* van Bath, *op. cit.*, pp. 145–151.
† van Bath, *op. cit.*, Part III, Chapters B and C.

2 ECONOMICS OF POST FEUDAL SOCIETY

The economic advantages of the demise of the manorial system would seem to be two.

1) Labor markets would be more highly organized, and
2) the capitalization of agriculture would proceed with greater speed.

Both of these gains would be minor, the second because of the nature of agricultural technology.* (Not until 1803 did Prussia find it desirable to abolish feudalism and encourage capital intensive agriculture; this event coincided with the scientific revolution of agriculture to which Prussia contributed.) Hence, the economic history of post feudal society should not differ from that of late feudalism.

The fifteenth century is much better documented than the fourteenth and the sixteenth is still better. Throughout Northwest Europe, before population reached its preplague level, wages seemed to hold more or less constant in terms of wheat but fell in terms of animal products and cattle. Hence, real wages fell slowly. After 1500, they fell quite rapidly. After 1500, terms of trade in England turned strongly in favor of agriculture. All this is in keeping with predictions in chapters 3 and 4. Looking only at cities, Lopez and Miskimim have characterized the 15th and 16th centuries as times of recession.† It would not be a recession in the modern sense of unemployment but certainly the towns deteriorated. (After 1600, the New World was as important alternative and real wages began to rise. In effect, the land of the European system was greatly enlarged so that the system was shifted back to a much earlier time except with equalization of rural-urban wage rates).

A reflection of economic conditions is afforded by population trends. Urban population should continue to decline or, as feudalism spreads, decrease as a proportion of rural population. Demographic scholarship based upon hearth and poll taxes vindicate that in Western Europe, except for Spain, total population increased after the black death until the middle of the 16th century, and the urban-rural population remained constant in

---

* *Ibid.* Opportunities for capital in agriculture prior to 1800 existed, but would appear limited according to Eric Kerridge, *The Agricultural Revolution*, Gorden Allen and Unwin, Ltd. (1967).

† Lopez and Miskimim, "Economic Depression of the Renaissance," *Economic History Review*, 14 (1962), 408–426.

Spain, Italy, Southern France, and the Low countries.* Some towns grew exceptionally fast, more than the normal 50% or so. Examples were Antwerp and London which at least doubled over 200 years.† On the other hand, in East Europe, where towns made up a much smaller percentage of the whole, population increased more rapidly than West Europe. Poland, East Germany, Bohemia, and Hungary made perhaps 10% of feudal European population in the mid 16th century whereas they were tribal in the mid 14th century.‡ Where there are comparable records of rural growth, fast growing towns were a small percentage of total towns and hence, the urban-rural ratio would seem to have fell slightly, in keeping with the theory.

In Tables 4 and 5 computations appear which yield the exact opposite conclusions due to the inclusion of East Europe in all periods. In Table 4, there are estimates of urban-rural population on the basis of the fragmentary data available on towns. The information on total national population is relatively respectable for England, Italy, Spain, Scandinavia and Switzerland (in Germany), the Low Countries and France but highly questionable for Germany and East Europe. In particular, for Germany the population of towns was used to extrapolate the whole on the basis of ratios found elsewhere. Since the late Middle Ages was a period of growth for Prussia and since its' one town, Danzig, doubled its population between 1350 and 1420, it is possible that the German population was somewhat larger in 1500 than indicated.

In general, the data shows exceptional growth of cities from 1340 to 1500 in four places, Flanders, Paris, London, and North Italy. All were areas dependent upon international trade. Hence, it may be that the establishment of East Europe as a source of grain to West Europe would yield a falling urban-rural population. Prior to 1340, East Europe with perhaps 10–12 million people was not a part of Feudal Europe as a whole, which had a population of 50 to 60 million. Hence, the total "European" population was unchanged, whereas urban population increased by about 25% (Table 4). In view of the decline of the Caliphate the decrease in urban population in Iberia may be understated. Also, the increase in England is based upon London alone, which may have grown faster than other English towns. Finally, the Italian figures are not reliable as representatives of urban population since no hard distinction was made between the towns and the

---

*   Russell, *Late Ancient and Medieval Population*, (Philadelphia, 1958, Transactions of the American Philosophical Society).
†   Russell, *op. cit.*
‡   M. M. Fryde, "The Population of Medieval Poland," appendix to Russell, *op. cit.*

The Economics of Feudalism

Table 4 Rural/Urban Population in Europe, 1–1500

(Source: Russell, Late Ancient and Medieval Population, Philadelphia, 1958, *Transactions of the American Philosophica Society* with appendix by M. M. Fryde).

	1	350	600	800	1000	1200	1340	1500
Greece & Balkins total pop.	5	5	3	5	5	4	4	4·5
rural/urban		17^2	10^2			17^2		13^2
Iberia total pop.	6	4	3.6	4	7	8	9.5	3.8
rural/urban	40			10^2			32	32
Gaul: total pop.	6.6	5	3	5				
rural/urban	40							
France and Low Cuntries total pop:					6	10	19	16
rual/urban							70^1	53^1
taly: total pop.	7.4	4	2.4	4	5	7.8	9.3	5.8
rural/urban		27^1				30^1	30^1	$13.^1$
Ger. & Scandinavia total pop.	3.5	3.5	2.1	4	4	7	11	7
rural/urban							50^1	23^1
British Isles: total pop.	.4	.3	.8	1.2	1.7	2.8	5.3	4
rural/urban	∞	∞	∞		100^1	100^1	76	30
East Europe: total pop.					9.5	9.2	11.2	10
rural/urban					100^1			100^2
Europe: total pop.	28.9	21.8	14.9	23.2	38.2	48.8	69.3	55.6

[1] Towns over 10,000
[2] Towns over 20,000

Table 5 Urban Population (thousands), 1340 and 1500

	1340	1500
France and Low Countries	270	300
Italy	350	670
Greece and Balkins	230[1]	300
Germany & Scandinavia	200	300
England	80	150
Iberia	300[2]	260[3]
TOTAL	1,540	1,980

[1] 1200 A. D.

[2] No data appears in Russell, *op. cit.*, except for Barcelon and Lisbon, however, 600–700, Muslim Spanish towns had 270,000 which have been halved and added to the Barcelona-Lisbon Total.

[3] Only Barcelona and Valencia are documented for 1500 and they showed a small decrease from 1340. Similar trends appear for small towns in Catalonia.

outlying areas.* For example, Sicily and the district around Naples grew by almost one half at a time when total population for Italy decreased. Yet it was in the North that the great growth of cities made the figure so high. Hence, it is possible that the population growth of Italy has been under estimated. Under estimation of the growth of total population in Germany and possibly Italy together with a possible over estimation of the growth of towns in England and Italy would account for the unexpected results of Table 4 and 5. For example, Bennett† estimates that European population increased from 51 million in 1350 (about Russell's 1200 figure) for Europe minus East Europe) to 69 million in 1500, a 40% increase which together with the 20% added by East Europe would give with an increase of about 60% on total population, which was certainly not matched by the growth of cities in Table 5. Even the rapid growth of towns may be suspect in view of the incidence of the plague in urban areas.

---

* The Italians estimated Antwerp to have 80–100,000 people in the 1506 whereas reference to local data shows that this was instead the population of the district of which Antwerp was the principle town. Instead, its population was perhaps 10,000 (Russell, *op. cit.*, p. 121).

† Bennett, *The Worlds' Food*, 1954.

For Product Safety Concerns and Information please contact our EU
representative GPSR@taylorandfrancis.com
Taylor & Francis Verlag GmbH, Kaufingerstraße 24, 80331 München, Germany

www.ingramcontent.com/pod-product-compliance
Ingram Content Group UK Ltd.
Pitfield, Milton Keynes, MK11 3LW, UK
UKHW021826240425
457818UK00006B/90